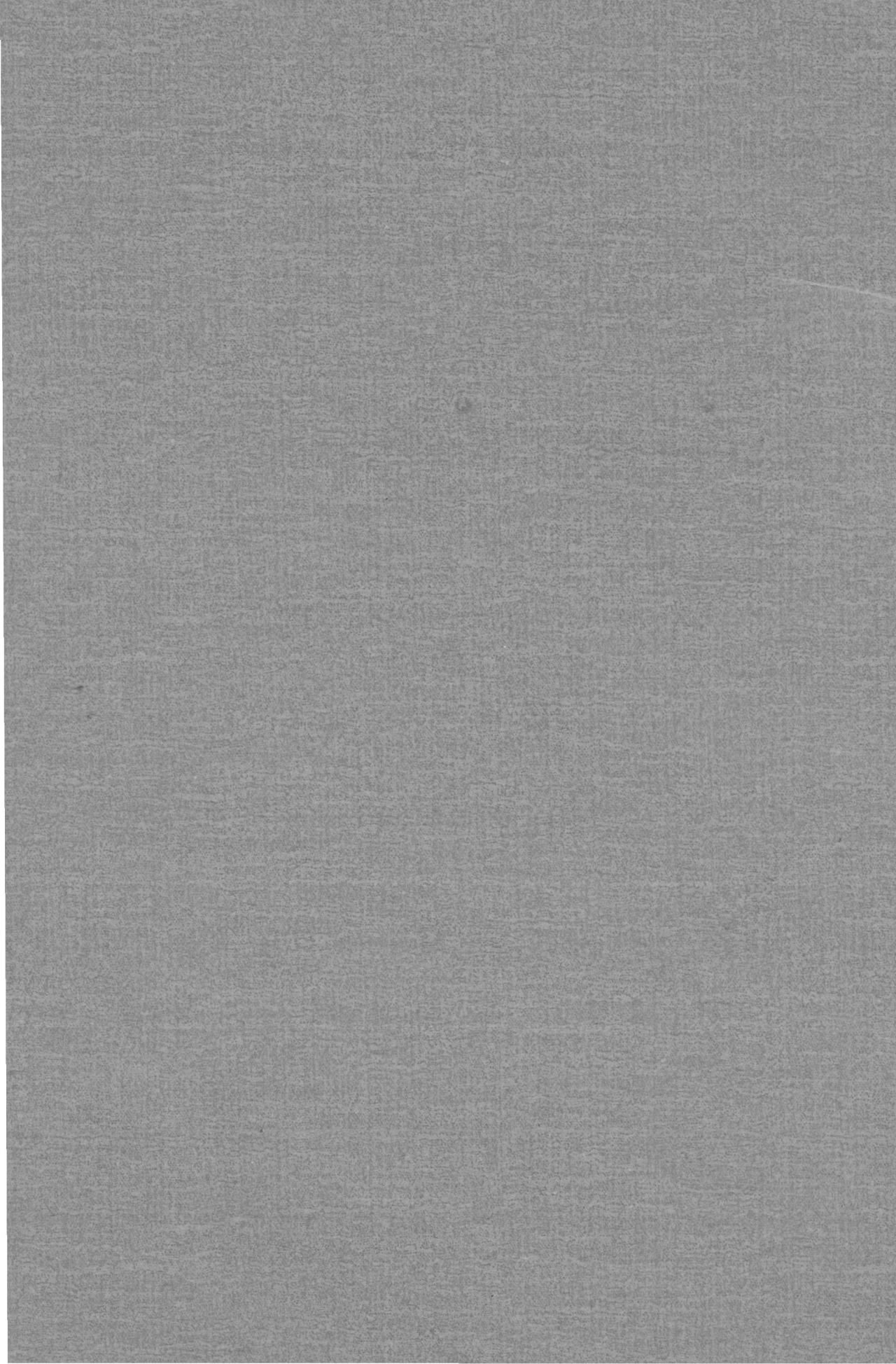

海外中華古籍書志書目叢刊

加拿大多倫多大學
慕氏藏書目（外一種）

4

加拿大多倫多大學 編
東亞圖書館
喬曉勤 主編

國家圖書館出版社

第四册目録

9

The University of Toronto Chinese Library

. . . .

Accession No. 1732   26   Index No. 055-8986

Title 硯山畢公年譜 *Yen Shan Pi Kung Nien Pu*

Classification ß-107

Subject

References

Author 清 史善長 撰 (*Written by*) (*Ching*), *Shih Shan-Chang*

Edition 家藏版 *Private-printed family edition*
同治年刻 竹紙 夾板 *bamboo paper, Wood-block*
Dated — Tung-Chih period 1862-1874

Index

Bound in 1 tao, 1 ts'ê

Remarks

1

The University of Toronto Chinese Library

. . . .

Accession No. 1733   Index No. 007 - b zkb

Title 井田圖攷 Ching Tien Tú Kǎo

Classification B — 282 政術 — 通志 (government and administration — general works)
          chéng shù   tung chih

Subject a general works of "Ching - Tien" system.

References

Author 清, 朱克己 訂定 (founded by) (Ching) Chu Ko-Chi

Edition 山東書局刊, 光緒年制, 連史紙 木板
      Shan-Tung Book Company. Kuang-Hsü period (1875-1908)
      "Lien-shih" paper, wood block

Index a general table of contents for 2 t'se.

Bound in 1 t'ao, 2 t'se

Remarks

2

The University of Toronto Chinese Library

．．．．．．．．．．．．．．．．．．．．．

Accession No. 64 1735   Index No. 070-dedぇ

Title 於越先賢像傳贊 Yü yüeh Hsien Hsien Hsiang Chuan Tsan

Classification B-117

Subject

References

Author 王齡撰 任渭長畫 Written by Wang Ling, Jen Wei-Chang

Edition 王氏敬和堂藏版 Wang-Shih, Ching-Ho-Tāng private-print
咸豐年刊 沈敦和藏 綿連紙 Ch'ēn-Tāng-Ho private library "Mien-Lien" paper
Dated — Hsien-Fēng period (1851-1861)

Index

Bound in 1 t'ao 2 ts'ǒ

Remarks

3

Accession No. *1736*   Index No. *030-63* 九

Title 古泉節錄 *Ku Pin Chieh Lu*

Classification *B-107* 傳記獨錄

Subject

References

Author 清松筠撰 *Written by* (*Ching*) *Sung Yün*

Edition 直隸重鑴 *Chih-Li reprinted*
道光二年重鑴 *dated Tao-Kuang 2 / 1822*

Index 錦連紙 *"Mien-Lien" paper*

Bound in *1 tào 6 chuan 6 táè*

Remarks

The University of Toronto Chinese Library

....

Accession No. 1737   Index No. 039.9889

Title 孫子十家註 Sun Tzŭ Shih Chia Chu

Classification C-33

Subject

References

Author 清 王詒壽等校 Collated by (Ching), Wang I Shou and others

Edition 光緒三年 浙江書局據孫氏平津本館本重校刊
Chechiang Book Co revised according to Sun-shih, Ping-Chin-Kuang edition

Dated — Kuang-Hsü "Ting-Chou" 3/1877

Index

Bound in 1 t'ao   6 ts'ü

Remarks

The University of Toronto Chinese Library
. . . .

Accession No. 1738   Index No. 170-hjjd

Title 陶樓文鈔 T'ao Lou Wên Ch'ao

Classification D

Subject

References

Author 清黃彭年撰 (Ch'ing) *Written by* Huang Pêng Nien

Edition 家藏版 Private-*family* printed edition

Index

Bound in 十四卷六冊 14 Chuan, 6 Ts'e

Remarks 光緒十四年刻 Block engraving in *the 14th year of* Kuang Hsü.
白紙 White Paper

6

The University of Toronto Chinese Library

....

Accession No. 1739   Index No. 149-iiee

Title 諸葛宗岳史四公文集　a. 諸葛忠武侯集　b. 宋宗忠简公集
　　　Chu Ko Tsung Yüeh Shih Ssŭ Kung Wên Chi　c. 岳忠武王集　d. 史忠正公集

Classification D-23　　　a. Chu Ko Wu Hou Chi　b. Sung Chung
　　　　　　　Chien Kung Chi　c. Yüeh Chung Wu Wang Chi　d. Shih Chung Chêng
Subject　　　　　　　　　　　　　　　　　　　　　　　　　　(Kung Chi)

References

Author a. 諸葛亮(三國)　c. 岳飛(宋)　　　清　劉質慧核刊
　　　　b. 宗澤(宋)　　d. 史可清(明)
　　　　(Ching) Liu Chih Hui (revised)　a. Chu Ko Liang (Three Kingdoms), b Tsung Tse (Sung)
Edition 同治十二年刊　　述荆堂藏書 c. Yüeh Fei (Sung) d. Shih Ko Fa
　　　　　　　　　　　　　　　　　　　　　　　　　　(Ming)
　　　Shu-Ching-Tang private library
　　　Dated — Tung-Chih "Kuei-yu" 12/1873

Index

Bound in 2 t'ao　　14 ts'ê

Remarks

The University of Toronto Chinese Library

. . . .

Accession No. 1741   Index No. 072-dx9x

Title 昆陵詩錄 K'un Ling Shih Lu

Classification D-38

Subject

References

Author 趙震轅清自雍乾間詩教古文詞作者
Compiled by Chao Chên
Edition 壬戌年刊
         Dated, Ching, Yung-Chêng and Chien Lung period 1723-1795

Index

Bound in 1 t'ao   4 ts'ê

Remarks

The University of Toronto Chinese Library
....

Accession No. 1742   Index No. 164-Kgc7

Title 鶚哈軒詩文集 I Su Hsüan Shih Wên Chi

Classification D—38 封集一詩

Subject An individual collection of poetry

References

Author 清, 弘銘 � (Ching), Kung Chao-Hsi

Edition 保合堂藏板, 道光丁亥年鐫, 綿連紙
~~block preserved~~
Pao-Ho-Tang edition, dated Tao-Kuang "Ting-Hai" /1827
"Mien-Lien" paper

Index None

Bound in 1 t'ao, 4 ts'ê

Remarks

The University of Toronto Chinese Library

. . . .

Accession No. 1743   Index No. 072-d c z a

Title 明名人尺牘小品 Ming Ming Jen Chih Tu
                                    Hsiao Pin
Classification 万

Subject

References

Author 清王元勳等輯 *Compiled by* (Ching) Wong Yüan Hsün

Edition 抱芳閣刊本 Pao Fang Kê Block-printing edition

Index

Bound in 四卷四冊 4 Chüan 4 Tsê

Remarks 光緒辛巳年刻 block-engraving in Kuang Hsü "Hsintzu"
         綿連紙 Mien-Lien paper.

10

The University of Toronto Chinese Library

....

Accession No. 1344   Index No. 085-lege

Title 潭柘山岫雲寺志 Tán Chê Shan Hsiu Yün Ssŭ Chih

Classification B一194 地理一刻志

Subject Local gazeteer of 潭柘山, 岫雲寺
                                      Tán Chê Shan, Hsiu Yün Ssŭ

References

Author 神穆張編訂 edited by Shên Mu-Tê

Edition 家藏版. 乾隆四年刻. 竹紙
        Private family [ ] edition, dated Chien-Lung 4/1739.   Bamboo paper

Index a general table of contents for 2 Chüan

Bound in 1 t'ao, 2 Chüan, 2 t'sê

Remarks

The University of Toronto Chinese Library
. . . .

Accession No. 1745   Index No. 031. 上海

Title 國朝詩法考 Kuo Chao Shih Fa Kao

Classification B— 702 傳記

Subject

References

Author 清, 趙鉞纂. Compiled by (Ching), Chao Yüeh

Edition 世美堂藏版, 道光辛卯年刊, 毛邊紙
Shih-Mei-Tang edition. (block preserved) dated Tao-Kuang "Hsin-Mao"/1831
"Mao-Pien" paper

Index none

Bound in 1 t'ao, 1 ts'ê

Remarks

12

The University of Toronto Chinese Library

. . . .

Accession No. 1746   Index No. 030-Lieg

Title 唱道真言 Chàng Tao Chên Yen

Classification C—731 (道教) Tao Chia (Taoism)

Subject Taoism

References

Author 青華道君太乙祖師聖製 Ching-Hua Tao-Wên-Tsu-Shih

Edition 虛静室藏版 (道光李刻) 杉代
Hsü-Ching-Shih, edition [block preserved], [Dated] Tao-Kuang period (1821-1850)
"fêng" paper

Index None

Bound in 1 tào, 5 chüan, 2 thê

Remarks

The University of Toronto Chinese Library

· ·

Accession No. 1747   Index No. 030-bmsz

Title 史學驪珠 Shih Hsüeh Li Chu

Classification B-367

Subject

References

Author 清 周贇著 (ching), Chou Yun

Edition 光緒七年刊
Dated,— Kuang-Hsü "Hsin-Ssŭ" 7/1881

Index

Bound in 1 táo   4 ts'ê

Remarks

The University of Toronto Chinese Library

. . . .

Accession No. *1749*   Index No. *111-caih*

Title   知本提綱 *Chih Pên Tí Kang*

Classification   *乙-158* 術義

Subject

References

Author   清楊厚著，鄭世鐸詳 *(Ching) Yang Hou* (書) *Chêng Shih-To* *Annotated by* (詳)

Edition   崇本齋版精刻本 *Chung-Pên Chai edition, fine printed copy*
          乾隆年刻 *dated Chien-Lung period (1736-1795)*
          夾連紙 *"Chia-Lien" paper*

Index

Bound in   *1 táo   10 chuan   10 tsê*

Remarks

. . . .

Accession No. 1750   Index No. 030-bze

Title 古文苑 Ku Wên Yuan

Classification 石

Subject

References

Author

Edition 飛青閣影 宋淳熙本
Photo-lithographic edition by Fei Ching Ke.

Index

Bound in 九卷三冊 9 Chuan 3 Ts'e

Remarks 清江楊氏家藏 (Ching) 江 Chiang Yang shih Private
         family edition
         光緒五年刊 Block engraving in the 5th year of Kuang Hsü
         錦連紙 "Mien-Lien" paper

16

The University of Toronto Chinese Library

. . . .

Accession No. 1751   Index No. 162-lebh

Title (箋)注六朝麗辭 Hsüan Chu Liu Cháo Táng Fu

Classification D—118 詞曲—詞(箋)

Subject Commentaries on selected Lyrics of 六朝
                                              Liu Cháo

References

                           Selected & Annotated by
Author 清, 馬傅康 箋注。(Ching) Ma Chuan-Kêng

Edition 京都松林齋刊本, 光緒丙子季刊, 印連紙
        Ching-Tu, Sung Lin-chai edition, dated Kuang-Hsü "Ping-Tzǔ"
                                                          1876
        "Mien-Lien" paper

Index a general table of content for 2 tsè

Bound in 1 táo, 2 tsè

Remarks

17

The University of Toronto Chinese Library

. . . .

Accession No. 1752   Index No. 067-3291

Title 文粹補萃 Wên Tsui Pu I

Classification 刀 — 75 總集一文

Subject a general collection of prose

References

Author 清 郭麇纂 (Ching) Kuo Lin
                Compiled by   Chiu

Edition 許氏榆園刊, 光緒年刊, 錦連張, 木版
        Hsü-Shih, Yü-Yüan edition, dated Kuang-Hsü Period (1875-1908)
        (Mien-Lien) 5 "Mien-Lien" paper, wood block.

Index a general table of contents for 26 chüan, a separate
        table of contents for each item.

Bound in 1 t'ao, 26 chüan, 4 ts'ê

Remarks

The University of Toronto Chinese Library

....

Accession No. 1753   Index No. 060-hhdj

Title 御製全韻詩 Yü Chih Chüan Yün Shih.

Classification D—68 詩集—評

Subject a general collection of poetry; with commentaries

References

Author 清彭元瑞恭錄 五十八
(Chʻing) Pʻêng yüan-jui reprinted edition
Edition 殿板, 綿連紙
Palace edition, "mien-lien" paper

Index Different rhyme for each 体; 上平声 Shang Ping Shêng
下平声, 上声, 去声, 入声.
Hsia Ping Shêng, Shang Shêng, Chü Shêng, Ju Shêng.
Bound in 1 函, 5 冊

Remarks

19

The University of Toronto Chinese Library
. . . .

Accession No. 1754   Index No. 160-i h i

Title 辨惑編 Pien Ho Pien

Classification C — 308 雜著 — 雜文

Subject ~~Tsta Chaia~~ — ~~Tsta~~ Wên (Miscellaneous writings)

References

Author 元. 謝應芳撰 (Written by) (Yüan) Hsieh Ying-Fang

Edition 四庫全書本, 守山閣叢書, 子部 竹紙
Ssŭ-Ku-Chüan-Shu Pên, Shou-Shan-Ko Tsúng Shu, Tzŭ Pu
Bamboo paper

Index an introduction include the contents for 4 Chüan

Bound in 1 T60, 4 Chüan, 2 thê

Remarks

20

The University of Toronto Chinese Library

· ·

Accession No. 1755   Index No. 167 076-Lec3

Title 欽定各郊壇廟樂章 *Chin Ting Ko Hsiao Tan Miao Yüeh Chang*

Classification C-228

Subject

References

Author 清 勵宗萬奉旨編 ~~edited by~~ *Ching, Li Tsung-Wan*

Edition 殿版 乾隆甲戌年刊 *Palace edition*
        Dated — Chien-Lung "Chia-Hsü" 19/1754

Index

Bound in 1 t'ao 2 ts'ê

Remarks

21

The University of Toronto Chinese Library

. . . .

Accession No. *1758*   Index No. *001-b3 < 3*

Title 三魚堂文集 *San Yü Táng Wēn Chi*

Classification *D-43*

Subject

References

Author 清 陸隴其著 *Chíng, Lu Lung-chi*

Edition 老掃葉山房藏板 *Lao-Sao-Yeh-Shan-Fang printed. block preserved ed.*

Index

Bound in *1 táo   8 tsʻè*

Remarks

The University of Toronto Chinese Library

. . . .

Accession No. 1759   Index No. 005.a3he

Title 九章算術細草圖說   附海島算經細草圖說
Chiu chang ~~Tsu~~ Suan Shu Hsi Tsao Tu Shao, Fu ~~Hai~~ Hai Tao Suan Ching
                                    Hsi Tsao Tu Shao
Classification C-138

Subject

References

Author 魏 劉徽注 唐 李淳風等注釋 清 李潢譔
Wei, Liu Hui; Tang, Li Chun-Feng and others (commentaries); Ching, Li Huang
Edition 清嘉慶"庚辰"新鎸 語鴻堂藏板 肆雅堂發兌
Yu-Hung-Tang private ed. Ssu-Ya-Tang
Dated — Ching, Chia-Ching "Kêng-Chên" 25/1820

Index

Bound in 1 t'ao   9 ts'ê

Remarks

23

The University of Toronto Chinese Library

. . . .

Accession No. 1760   Index No. 096-3bed

Title 王右丞集箋註 Wang Yu Chêng Chi Chien Chu

Classification D-43 D-63

Subject

References

                              Compiled & coll copied by
Author 清 趙殿成輯錄, Ch'ing, Chao Tien-Chêng

Edition

Index

Bound in 1 t'áo   8 ts'ê'

Remarks

The University of Toronto Chinese Library

. . . .

Accession No. *1762*   Index No. *048-b272,*

Title 左传掇遗 *Tso Chuan Shih I*
     傳

Classification *A—101* 春秋左传

Subject

References

Author 清, 朱师辙著 *Ching, Chu Shih-Hui*

Edition 家藏版, 竹纸, 木版

Private family ✻ Home edition, Bamboo paper, wood block

Index *None*

Bound in / 套, 2 册

Remarks

Accession No. *1763*　　　　Index No. ~~MB 0~~ 118-03 L3

Title 稽厓高遺文
　　　Chou Kao Yi Wěn

Classification D—43 別集一文

Subject *an individual collection of miscellaneous prose writings & letters.*

References

Author 清 諸暨逸者，陳淳輯
　　　Ching, Sun Yi Jao,　Compiled by Chén Chun.

Edition 歸安穎川書舍刊，民國十五年印 平紛連紙
　　　Jui-An, Ying-Chüan-Shu-Shê edition
　　　Dated Republic 15/1926.　"Ping-Fên-Lien" paper

Index *A general table of contents for 2 Chüan*

Bound in *1 t'ao, 2 Chüan, 2 tsê*

Remarks

The University of Toronto Chinese Library

. . . .

10

Accession No. *1764*   Index No. *123-99* ᶜᵉ

Title 羣經字詁 *Chün Ching Tzǔ Ku*

Classification *A-137*

Subject

References

Author 清 段譯廷原稿 黃本驥編訂
Ching Tuan. O-Ting (original draft), Huang Pēn-Chi (edited)
Edition 黔陽楊氏存版 *Chien-Yang, Yang-shih private ed.*
光緒乙酉年刊 毛邊紙 *"Mao-Pien" paper*
Dated — Kuang-Hsü period 1875 - 1908

Index

Bound in *2 t'ao   12 chuan   16 ts'ê*

Remarks

The University of Toronto Chinese Library

. . . .

Accession No. ~~12~~ 1765   Index No. 039. c ~~c~~ 28 l

Title 字典考證 Tzŭ Tien Kǎo Chêng

Classification A-161

Subject

References

Author 清 奕繪等輯錄 Compiled & Copied by Ching, I Hui and others

Edition 進呈本 愛日堂藏本 Ai-Jah-Tʻang private ed.
Presented to the Throne.
毛邊紙 "Mai-Pien" paper

Index

Bound in 1 tʻao   8 tsʻê

Remarks

28

The University of Toronto Chinese Library

. . . .

Accession No. 1767   Index No. 085-9ㅗㅗㄴㄷ

Title 海國圖志, Hai Ko Tu chih

Classification B-227

Subject

References

Author 魏源撰, *Written by* Wei Yüan

Edition 光緒六年邵陽急當務齋新鎸
Shao-Yang, Chi-Tang-Wu-Chai
Dated — Kuang-Hsü "Keng-Chên" 6/1880

Index

Bound in 4 tao, 24 ts'ê (6 each)

Remarks

29

The University of Toronto Chinese Library

. . . .

Accession No. 1768   Index No. 046-399h

Title 山海經箋疏 Shan Hai Ching Chien Su

Classification C-510

Subject

References

Author 晉 郭璞傳 清 阮元校刊
Chin, Kuo Pu-Chuan, Ching, Juan, Yüan (revised)

Edition 嘉慶己巳年 阮氏琅嬛仙館開雕
Juan-Shih, Lang-Huan-Hsien-Kuang

Dated — Chia-Ching "Chi-I" 14/1809

Index

Bound in 1 táo.   4 tsê'

Remarks

The University of Toronto Chinese Library

. . . .

Accession No. *1269 1 冊*   Index No. 041. *8883*

Title 封氏聞見記 *Fêng Shih Wên Chien Chi*

Classification 乙 — 308 雜文

Subject *miscellaneous writings*

References

Author 唐, 封演 *Tʻang, Fêng Yen*

Edition 雅雨堂版、迪莊辦、竹紙、木板
Ya-Yü-Tʻang edition, Ti-Chuang edition,
Bamboo paper, wood block

Index *a general table of contents for 10 chüan*

Bound in *1 tʻao, 10 chüan, 2 tsʻê*

Remarks 與亡名氏雜錄合裝盛一套內
Bound with "Wên Chang Tsa Lu"

The University of Toronto Chinese Library

. . . .

Accession No. 1969 B.   Index No. 067-3dgh

Title 文昌雜錄 Wên Cháng Tsa Lu

Classification 乙—308 雜文

Subject miscellaneous writings

References

Author 清, 龐元英著 Ching. Páng Yüan-Ying

Edition 雅雨堂版, 乾隆年刻, 竹紙
Ya-Yü-Táng edition
Dated Chien-Lung period (1736-1795)
Bamboo paper

Index a general table

Bound in 1 t'ao, 6 chüan, 2 t'sê

Remarks 5 封元閣見沉存裝于一套内

The University of Toronto Chinese Library

. . . .

Accession No. 1771   Index No. 018-8898

Title 剑舞幕法. Chih I Tsung Hua

Classification

D - 95 試文

Subject ?

References

Author 清. 津梁章鉅撰. Written by Ching, Liang Chang-Chü

Edition 知足知不足齋本, 光緒辛巳年刻, 竹纸

Chih Tsu-Chih-Pu-Tsu-Chai edition
Dated Kuang-Hsü Hsin-Sïu 1881
Bamboo paper

Index none

Bound in 1 套, 24 chüan, 8 tsê

Remarks

The University of Toronto Chinese Library
....

Accession No. 1773   Index No. 077-1cbh

Title 歷代史論 (山曉閣重訂歷代史論) Li Tai Shih Lun (Shan Hsiao
                                              Ko Chung Ting Li Tai Shih Lun)

Classification B-367

Subject

References

Author 清 張孫執升評定 張西銘原著史論
        Ching, Sun Chih Shêng (annotations), Chang Hsi-Ming
Edition ● 康熙年刻 金閶龔晉之梓行 茅九刻
        Ching-Chêng, Kung-Chin-Chih Nine edition
        Dated — Kang-Hsi period 1622—1722

Index

Bound in 2 táo. 8 ts'è

Remarks

The University of Toronto Chinese Library

....

Q6

Accession No. 1774   Index No. 040-mcbc

Title 寰宇分合志, Huan Yü fên Ho Chih

Classification B42

Subject

References

Author 明　徐樞編輯, edited & Compiled by Ming, Hsü Shu

Edition 湘潭楊氏家藏縮本 Hsiam-Tan, Yang-Shih private family ed.
光緒二十八年印　毛太紙 "Mao-Tai" paper
Dated — Kuang-Hsü "Jên-Ying" 28/1902

Index

Bound in 1 táo   9 chuan   8 ts'ǎ

Remarks

35

Accession No. *1775*   Index No. *140-iid8*

Title 萬善花室文蒿 *Wan Shan Hua Wu Wên Kao*

Classification *D-43*

Subject

References

Author 方履籛著 *Fang Lü-Chien*

Edition 用道光己丑刊本重雕
Re-printe p. from "Tao-Kuang, "Chi-Chou" 8/1829 ed.

Index

Bound in *1 t'áo   3 ts'ê*

Remarks

The University of Toronto Chinese Library
....

Accession No. 1776   Index No. 064-9kkp

Title 振綺堂叢書初集 Chen I Tang Tsun Shu Chu Chi

Classification C-338

Subject

References

Author 清 汪康年撰諸家著作∧^written by Ching, Wang Kang-Nien (edited)

Edition 宣統年 汪氏印 Wang-shih printed
        Dated — Hsüan-Tung period 1909-1911

Index

Bound in

Remarks

The University of Toronto Chinese Library

. . . .

45

Accession No. 1777   Index No. 077- ℓcℓℓ

Title 歷代帝王统系 Li Tai Ti Wang Tʻung Hsi

Classification B -157

Subject

References

Author 清 夏元閞原編　傅吉爭删訂
Originally edited by Chʻing, Hsia Yüan Kʻai; Fu Chü Chêng (revised)

Edition 于時亭藏版 聿修堂 Yü-Shih-Ting private ed.
雲雅堂藏 Yü-Hsiu-Tang block preserved ed.
Hsüeh-Ya-Tang preserved

Index

Bound in

Remarks

The University of Toronto Chinese Library

. . . .

Accession No. 1778   Index No. 005-ajjd

Title 九水山房文存 Chiu Shui Shan Fang Wên Tsun

Classification D-43

Subject

References

Author 清 畢亨著 (九水先生) Ching, Pi Hêng (Chiu Shui Hsien Shêng)

Edition 咸豐二年刊

　　　　Dated — Hsien-Fêng "jên-tzu" 2/1852

Index

Bound in 1 táo 1 tsạ̈

Remarks

The University of Toronto Chinese Library

....

Accession No. *1779*   Index No. *053-Lchg*

Title 庸吏庸言 *Yung Li Yung Yen*

Classification *C — 308* 朝蒙 — 朝文

Subject *miscellaneous writings of the work of the county government to the people*

References

Author 清, 刘衡撰 稿 *Chíng, Liu Héng Ppreserved draft.*

Edition 家藏版, 绵连纸
Private family stone edition, "Mien-Lien" paper

Index *a general table of contents for 2 tsé*

Bound in */ tào, 2 tsé*

Remarks

The University of Toronto Chinese Library
....

Accession No. 1780   Index No. 001-a3dd

Title 一山房集陶 I Shan Fang Chi Tao

Classification D 一38 别集一诗

Subject An individual collection of poetry with
commentary of 陶渊明
Tao Yüan-Ming

References

Author 清 清素主人著 Ching, Ching-Su-Chu-jên

Edition 写刻版. 光绪年刻, 绵连纸
Private family edition, dated Kuang-Hsü period (1875-1908), "Mien-Lien" paper

Index a general table of contents for 2 chüan

Bound in 1 t'ao, 2 Chüan, 2 册 tse

Remarks

The University of Toronto Chinese Library

. . . .

Accession No. 1781   Index No. 120-C7

Title 越書 Yüeh Shu

Classification 乙一308 雜家一雜文 (Miscellaneous Writing)
                          Tsa Chia   Tsa Wên

Subject miscellaneous writings of 信義
                                    "Hsin I"

References

Author 清. 謝智樹撰. Written by, Ching. Hsieh Chieh Shu

Edition 家藏版, 道光甲辰用鹍
Private family flame edition, dated Tao-Kuang "Chia-Chên"/1844

Index a general table of contents for 12 Chüan

Bound in 1 t'ao, 12 Chüan, 4 ts'e

Remarks

The University of Toronto Chinese Library

. . . .

Accession No. *1782 A* ~~*B*~~.   Index No. *o56-chi*

Title 梁子陸篇 *二右編* *Shih Ku Pien*

Classification 乙-308 雜文

Subject

References

Author 清, 莊璐轉, *Compiled by* *Ching, Chuàng Yao*

Edition 后有饒齋存版, 道光戊戌年刊. 毛邊紙
Liu-Yu-Yü-Chai edition, dated Tao-Kuang "Wu-Hsü" 1838.
"Mao-Pien" paper.

Index *none*

Bound in *1 tao. 5 chüan, 2 tsé*

Remarks 5 "梁子陸篇同卷子一套內
裝"

43

The University of Toronto Chinese Library

. . . .

Accession No. 1782 B.   Index No. 149-23 m 3

Title ~~未有~~ 課子隨筆 *Kó Tzǔ Sui Pi*

Classification C—308

Subject *collection from 70 ~~another~~ authors of homiletical writings*

References

Author 清, 張師載輯, *Compiled by* *Ching, Chang Shih-Tsai*

Edition 自有鐵齋存版, 道光癸卯手重樣, 毛邊紙
Liu-Yu-Yü-Chai, preserved edition, dated Tao-Kuang "Mao ~~Kuei-Mao~~/1843, Kuei
"Mao-Pien" paper

Index ~~none~~

Bound in 1 tàu, 10 chüan, 4 tsè

Remarks 5 寸 右係同著于一套內

The University of Toronto Chinese Library

. . . .

Accession No. *6* 1783   Index No. 082-3829

Title 毛詩辨韻 *Mao Shih Pien Yün*

Classification A-31

Subject

References

Author 清 趙似祖撰 *Written by* *Ching, Chao Ssŭ-Tsu*

Edition 家藏 *private family-printed*

綿連紙 夾板 *"Mien-lien" paper Wood-block*

Index

Bound in 1 tao, 4 ts'ê

Remarks

The University of Toronto Chinese Library

．．．．．．．．．．．．．．．．．．．．．．

6 (see p 1, 1654?)

Accession No. 1785   Index No. 120-gcaj

Title 經字正蒙 Ching Tzŭ Cheng Mêng

Classification A-161

Subject

References

                    Compiled by
Author 清 李文沂纂 Ching, Li Wên-I

Edition 粵東萃經堂刊本 Yueh-Tung, Ts'ui-Ching-Tang publish
光緒乙酉年刊 毛邊紙 "Mao-Pien" paper
Dated — Kuang-Hsü "I-yu" 11/1885

Index

Bound in 1 tao, 8 chuan, 8 ts'ê

Remarks

46

The University of Toronto Chinese Library

．．．．．．．．．．．．．．．．．．．．．．．．．．．

Accession No. 1787   Index No. 040-du

Title 宋豔 Chu Yen

Classification 乙—308 雜家—雜文 (Miscellaneous writing)
                        Tsa-chia Tsa-wen

Subject Miscellaneous writing of "Sung" dynasty

References

Author 清，徐士鑾 輯 Compiled by ching, Hsü Shih-Luan

Edition 鐵園藏版， preserved 光緒辛卯之冬/ Tieh-Yüan edition, Dated Kuang-Hsü "Hsin-Mao" winter/1891

Index a general table of contents for 12 chüan and every two seperate table of contents for 2 chüan (1 tsè)

Bound in 1 t'ao, 12 chüan, 6 tsè

Remarks

The University of Toronto Chinese Library
. . . .

Accession No. 1988   Index No. 037-22kz

Title 寄傲風廬詩集 Chi Ku Chin Shih Chi

Classification D—38 別集一詩

Subject An individual collection of poetry

References

Author 清, 葉昌熾 Written by, Ching, Yeh Chang-Chih

Edition 家藏版, 竹紙
Private family Home edition, Bamboo paper

Index none

Bound in 1 t'ao, 5 chüan, 5 t'ie

Remarks

The University of Toronto Chinese Library

· ·

Accession No. 1789   Index No. 030-bfj

Title 古詩源 Ku shih Yuan

Classification D

Subject

References

Author 清沈德潛選 *Selected by* Ch'ing, Shen Te Chien.

Edition 竹嘯軒藏版

Chu Hsiao Hsüan block preserved edition

Index

Bound in 十四卷六冊   14 Chüan, 6 Tsê

Remarks 竹紙 Bamboo paper

The University of Toronto Chinese Library

....

Accession No. 1790   Index No. 140-93 c

Title 莊子因 Chuang Tzŭ Yin

Classification e-731

Subject

References

Author 清 林雲銘評述 ∧ <u>Commented & given in oral by</u> Ch'ing, Lin Yün-Ming

Edition 乾隆二年蔡廬谷重刻 輔仁堂藏板
∖ Pu-Jên T'ang <s>private — printed</s> <u>blocks-preserved</u> edition, Ts'ai-Hsu-Ku <s>seco.</s> second ed.
Dated — Ch'ien-Lung "Ting-Ssŭ" 2/1737

Index

Bound in 1 t'ao   6 ts'ê

Remarks

50

The University of Toronto Chinese Library
....

Accession No. 1791   Index No. 037— apfp
Title 天蘇閣叢刊二集 T'ien ~~su~~ Su Ko Tsung K'an
Classification   Erh Chih

Subject

References

Author 清徐振飛輯 *Compiled by,* Ch'ing, Hsü Chen Fei
Edition 中華書局聚珍仿宋版
        Chung Hua Book Co. Chü-chên-Fang-Sung Printed.

Index

Bound in 六冊   6 Tée
Remarks 共十本種 白竹紙 White Bamboo paper.
        夾板 Wooden block.

The University of Toronto Chinese Library

. . . .

Accession No. 1792 4

Index No. 039 · cd $h

Title 宇林攷逸 *Tzŭ Lin Kǎo I*

Classification A-161

Subject

References

Author 清 任大椿 學 *Leaned by* *Chíng, Jen Ta-chün*

Edition 江蘇書局刊印本 *Chiang-Su Book Co. published ed.*
光緒庚寅年刊 綿連紙 夾版 *"Mien-Lien" paper*
Dated — *Kuang-Hsü "Kêng-Ying" 16/1890* *Wood-block*

Index

Bound in 1 tao, 8 chuan, 3 ts'ê

Remarks

The University of Toronto Chinese Library

· ·

Accession No. 1793   Index No. 040-9 9 b h

Title 容城三賢文集 Yung Cheng San Hsien Wen Chih

Classification 丙

Subject

References

Author 明,劉因,楊繼盛,孫奇逢 撰 Written by Ming, Liu Yin, Yang Chi Sheng, Sun Ch'i Feng.

Edition 俞廷獻重修本 Yü Ting Hsien revised edition

Index

Bound in 十二冊 12 Tsé

Remarks 光緒戊戌年刊 Kuang-Hsü "Wu Hsü" block-engraving.
毛边紙 Mao Pien paper
夾板 wooden block

The University of Toronto Chinese Library

. . . .

40

Accession No. 1794   Index No. 149- 06¼c

Title 讀史節要 *Tu Shih Chieh Yao*

Classification β-22

Subject

References

Author 清 汪承鏞輯。 *Compiled by Ch'ing, Wang Chêng-Yung*

Edition 家藏版 *private-printed family edition*

同治五年刻 綿連紙 夾板 *"Mien-Lien" paper*
丙寅   *Wood-block*
Index Dated — Tung-Chih "Ping-Ying" 5/1866

Bound in 1 t'ao   12 chuan   6 ts'i

Remarks

The University of Toronto Chinese Library
. . . .

Accession No. 1795   Index No. 001-bg2d

Title 上海租界问题 Shanghai Tsu Chieh Wên Ti

Classification B-303 雜誌 国際公法

Subject a historical, geographical, economical, political + social background of the "foreign concession" in Shanghai

References

Author 王挺唐挺, Written by Wang Chi-Táng [I]

Edition 縮珍仿宋印書句印
        Chü-Chên-Fang-Sung-Yin-Shu-Chü printed

Index a general table of contents for 3 Chüan

Bound in 1 t/20 3 Pei Chüan, 1 Tác

Remarks

The University of Toronto Chinese Library

. . . .

Accession No. *1796 A.*   Index No. *194-22 bi*

Title 魏郑公諫錄 *Wei chêng Kung chien Lu*

Classification ß—72 流公奏議一奏議

Subject

References

Author 唐, 王方慶·集, 王先春·校注

    Táng, Wang Fang-ching's collection, Wang Hsien-Kung ~~revised~~ *Collated & Commented, revised*

Edition 長沙王氏乘版 克清手刊, 綿連纸

    Chang-Sha, Wang-Shih's edition (block preserved) *Kuang-Hsü Period "Mien-Lien" paper*

             (1875-1908)

Index *a general table of contents for 3 Chüan*

Bound in *1 t'ao, 5 Chüan, 2 t'sê*

Remarks

The University of Toronto Chinese Library

....

Accession No. 1396 B.   Index No. ん zbb

Title 魏文莊公故事拾遺 Wei Wên Chên Kung Ku Shih Shih I

Classification β— 孔孟含秦集 秦時
117 13 记 一 鐵鐵

Subject collected biographies

References

Author 清, 王先謙 集 Ch'ing, Wang Hsien-Kung's collection

Edition 長沙王氏府林 光緒年刻 綿連紙
Chang-Sha Wang-Shih's edition Kuang-Hsü Period, "Mien Lien" paper
block preserved dated (1875-1908)

Index a general table of contents for 3 chüan

Bound in 1 t'ào, 3 chüan, 附年譜 1 chüan, 2 t'ào

Remarks Attached with "Nien-Pu" is attached

The University of Toronto Chinese Library

. . . .

4

Accession No. *1797*   Index No. *042- e 7 ac*

Title 尚書札記 *Shang Shu Tsa Chi*

Classification *A-21*

Subject

References

Author 清 許鴻磐 著 *ching, Hsü Hung-Pán*
        Hsüch-Hai-Tong private ed.   Huang-Ching-Ching
Edition 學海堂藏版 皇清經解本
        Hsüeh Hai Tong block preserved
        夾連紙 *"Chia-Lien" paper*

Index

Bound in *1 tao, 4 chuan, 4 ts'ê*

Remarks

58

Accession No. 1798   Index No. 001-dgig

Title 世說新語 三卷附錄四種 Shih Shuo Hsin Yü
                                    Erh Chüan Fu Lu Ssu Chung

Classification c-368

Subject

References

Author 宋 臨義慶撰 梁 劉孝標注
                         劉
Written by Sung, Wang I-Ching. Liang, Liu Kao (commentaries)
Edition 清光緒十七年思賢講舍開離
           Ssŭ-Hsien-Chiang-Shê
           Dated — Ching, Kuang-Hsü "Hsin-Mao" 17/1891

Index

Bound in 1 t'ao   6 ts'ê

Remarks

59

The University of Toronto Chinese Library

. . . .

Accession No. 1799   Index No. 128. Pjz

Title 聽園文存 Ting Yüan Wên Tsun

Classification 179. D-43

Subject

References

Author 張學尹撰 *Written by* Chang Hsüch-Yin

Edition 同治壬申 師白山房校刊 *collected*
Shih-pai-Shan-Fang revised ed.
Dated — Tung-chih "Jěn-Shang" 11/1872

Index

Bound in 1 tʿáo 4 tsʿê

Remarks

60

The University of Toronto Chinese Library

....

Accession No. 1800   Index No. 067 文苑d

Title 文苑珠林 Wên Yüan Chu Lin

Classification △

Subject

References

Author 清蔣超伯輯 *Compiled by* Ch'ing, Chiang Ch'ao Po

Edition 雲樂山房藏版 Yün Le San Fang block preserved edition

Index

Bound in 二卷二冊 2 Chuan, 2 Tsé

Remarks 連史紙 Mien-Lien Paper

61

The University of Toronto Chinese Library

· ·

18

Accession No. 1801   Index No. 046-dk kb

Title 岑襄勤公年譜 *Tsén Hsiang Lo Kung Nien Pu* <small>chin</small>

Classification β-107

Subject

References   *edited & compiled by*

Author 清 岑毓英 趙範 編輯 ∧ *Ching, Tsén Yü-Ying; Chao Fan*

Edition 家藏版 *Private family edition*
綿連紙 光緒己亥年刻刊
"Mien Lien" paper

Index

Bound in 1 Tao, 5 Ts'é, 10 Chuan

Remarks

62

The University of Toronto Chinese Library

. . . .

Accession No. 1802   Index No. -074-zchi

Title " Yüeh ling sui pien "
月   令   粹   編

Classification β-157 時令

Subject -(Wylie)- "..... is a compilation of historical memoranda
for every day in the year......"

References - Wylilie's Notes page 43   Gest No. 153. Toronto Nos. 504, 593
⌐1134

Author - by chin chia-mo 秦嘉謨

Edition

Index   a general table of contents for 卷 首 and 24 chüan

Bound in 1 t'ao 6 tiě

Remarks

63

The University of Toronto Chinese Library

· ·

Accession No. *1803*   Index No. *031-hci*

Title 四存編 *Ssŭ Tsun Pien*

Classification *C —— ?13* 儒家

Subject *?*

References

Author 明. 顏元著 *Ming. Yen Yüan*

Edition 家藏版. 康熙年刊. 毛邊紙
Private family edition, dated Káng-Hsi period (1662-1722)
"Mao-Pien" paper

Index *a separately [~~formal~~] table of contents for each section*
(all together 46 sections ——
存治編, 存人編   存性編, 存學編

Bound in *11 冊, 11 chüan, 2 函*   *Tsun Hsing Pien, Tsun Hsüeh Pien*

Remarks *Tsun Chih Pien, Tsun Jên Pien*

64

The University of Toronto Chinese Library

. . . .

Accession No. *1804*   Index No. *024.9293*

Title   南華經解   *Nan Hua Ching Chieh*

Classification *C-731*

Subject

References

Author   清 宣穎著   *Ching, Hsüan Ying*

Edition   康熙六十年刊   *Block-engraving in sixty year of "Kang-Hsi"*

Index

Bound in   *1 Táo   3 Tsʼè*

Remarks

The University of Toronto Chinese Library

. . . .

Accession No. *1805*   Index No. *145·9×3ᶜ*

Title 補藝文志五種 *Pu I Wên Chih Wu Chung*

Classification *B337* 史部 一目錄

Subject

References

Author 上元倪燦撰 *Written by* *Shang-Yüan,* *Ni* *Tsan*

Edition

光緒辛卯秋 廣雅書局刊

Dated Kuang-Hsü & "Hsin-Mao" /1891, Kuang-Ya Book

Index *company printed*

none

Bound in

1 tao, 5 tsl, 5 chüan

Remarks

The University of Toronto Chinese Library

· ·

Accession No. *1806*   Index No. *075- Lphm*

Title 棣懷堂隨筆 *Ti Huai Tang Sui Pi*

Classification *D-23*

Subject

References

Author 清 李象鵾著 *Ching, Li Hsiang-Kun*

Edition

Index

Bound in *1 Tao   4 Ts'o*

Remarks

The University of Toronto Chinese Library

....

Accession No. *1808*   Index No. *037-3233*

Title 大清一統輿圖 *Ta Ching I Tung Yü Tu*

Classification *B-232*

Subject

References

Author

Edition 同治二年鐫
板藏湖北撫署景桓樓
~~Pang Fang~~ *Hu-Pei, Fu Shu Ching Huan Lou Library*

Index

Bound in *2 Tao, 23 Ts'ê*

Remarks

The University of Toronto Chinese Library

....

Accession No. 1810   Index No. 057-babj

Title 弘正四傑詩集 *Hung Chêng Ssŭ Chieh Shih Chi*

Classification D-38

Subject

References

Author 明 李空同 何大復 徐迪功 邊華泉著 清張雨珊輯
       Ming, Li Kung-Tung, Ho Ta-fu, Hsü Ti-Kung, Pien Hua-Chüan, Ching, chang
Edition 光緒 "乙未" 年長沙張氏湘雨樓鏝板   *Yü-Shan.*
       , Chang-Sha, Chang-Shih, Hsiang Yü Lou

Index

Bound in 2 *T'ao*   16 *Ts'ê*

Remarks

The University of Toronto Chinese Library

....

Accession No. *1811*   Index No. *030. ed*

Title 周易 *Chou I*

Classification *A-11*

Subject

References

Author 宋 朱熹本義 *Sung, Chu Hsi*

Edition 摹宋刻大字 *Large character edition.*

宋咸淳乙丑吳革原刊本 綿連紙
Wu Ko original copy   "Mien Lien" paper

Index

Bound in *1 Tao. 2 Tsê*

Remarks

The University of Toronto Chinese Library

. . . .

22

Accession No. 1812   Index No. 031-bjic

Title 四裔編年表 Ssŭ I Pien Nien Piao

Classification B-147

Subject

References

Author 美國林樂知 中國嚴良勲同譯 清 李鳳苞彙編
Ch'ing, Li Fêng Pao; Lin & Lo-Chih (American), and Yen Liang-Hsün & translated 之
Edition 原刻本 originally block-print edition.
綿連紙 "Mien Lien" paper

Index

Bound in   1 T'ao   4 Ts'ê

Remarks

The University of Toronto Chinese Library

....

Accession No. 20 1814   Index No. 076-えとんら

Title 欽定國史忠義傳 Chin Ting Kuo Shih Chung I Chuan

Classification β-117

Subject

References

Author

Edition 抄寫本 manuscript
        硃色格 開化紙
        paper made in "Kai Hua" paper
Index   lithographic edition.

Bound in 2 Tao   25th. to 38th. chuan   14 Ts'ǝ

Remarks

Accession No. 1817   Index No. 010-d238

Title 光緒二十年奉天全省府廳州縣地輿圖志,
    Kuang Hsü Êrh Shih Nien Fêng Tien Ch'üan Shêng Fu T'ing Chou Hsien Ti Yü Tu Chih

Classification B-232

Subject

References

Author 王志修 編輯并校刊 *edited & compiled by Wang Chih-Hsiu*

Edition 國史館 *Kuo Shih Kuang*
        光緒二十年

Index

Bound in 1 T'ao, 1 Ts'ê

Remarks

The University of Toronto Chinese Library

. . . .

Accession No. *1818*　　　　　Index No. *104-333c*

Title 瘞鶴銘張補工 *Ho Ming Kao Pu*

Classification B 52 雜史

Subject

References

Author 清翁方綱撰 *Written by* *Ching, Wêng Fang-Kang*

Edition

硃印本 *Printed in Red edition*
連綿紙 *"Mien-lien" -"Lien" paper*

Index

Bound in *1 tao 2 tse*

Remarks

74

The University of Toronto Chinese Library

. . . .

Accession No. 1820   Index No. 140·idze   yu

Title 萬全圖要述 Wan ~~chin~~ ~~yo Hsia chi~~ Wan Ch'uan 圖 Hsia

~~chian li kuang~~

Classification と——158 術數

Subject miscellaneous writings of divination ; with
pictures

                                           divination

References

Author

Edition 素雲道人重印, 油光紙
    Su-Yün-Tao-Jen reprinted
    "Yu-Kuang" paper

Index a general table of content for 1 t'ao

Bound in 1 t'ao, 1 ts'e

Remarks

The University of Toronto Chinese Library

. . . .

Accession No. 1821   Index No. 085-gdll

Title 流沙墜簡 Liu Sha Chui Chien

Classification B-338

Subject

References

Author 羅振玉 編 _edited by_ Lo Chên-Yü

Edition 宣統甲寅年   上虞羅氏宸翰樓 印
Shang-Yü, Lo-Shih, Chên-Han-Lou

Index

Bound in 1 Táo 3 Tsǒ

Remarks

The University of Toronto Chinese Library

. . . .

Accession No. *1824*   Index No. *077·ndki*

Title 歸雲樓題畫詩 *Kuei Yün Lou Ti Hua Shih*

Classification *D—38 刻 第一卷*

Subject *an individual collection of poetry*

References

Author 清, 繡世白撰 *written by* *Ching, Hsü Shih-Chang*

Edition 世繡堂藏版, 連史紙
Chin-Hsiu-Tang edition, "Lien-Shih" paper *Preserved*

Index *none*

Bound in *1 t*ᵃᵒ*, 2 Chüan, 2 tsü*

Remarks

The University of Toronto Chinese Library
· ·

Accession No. *1825*   Index No. *118-i333*

Title 傳寫本老子 *Chuan Wên Lao Tzŭ*

Classification *C — D31 (道家) Tao Chia (Taoism)*

Subject *Taoism — "Lao-Tze"*

References

Author 田林侯秀 *Tien Fu-Hou* Copied by

Edition 呂蘇版 華宣紙
private family home edition, "Tau Hsüan" paper

Index *None*

Bound in *1 t'ao, 1 ts'e*

Remarks

The University of Toronto Chinese Library

. . . .

Accession No. 1826   Index No. 140-33

Title 荒書 *Huang Shu*

Classification B-32 史記事本末   "Shu Kuo"

Subject *a complete historical narratives of* 蜀國

References

Author 清，費密編次 *edited in order by* ^ *Ching, Fei Mi*

Edition 虔顧叢書本, 仿宋精刻, 毛邊紙 *Chien-Ching Tsung Shu Pên, unannotated Sung, fine printed edition, "Mao-Pien" paper*

Index *none*

Bound in / t'ao, / Tsê

Remarks

The University of Toronto Chinese Library

. . . .

Accession No. 1827   Index No. 072-de九系e

Title 明季國初進士履歷跋後 Ming chi Kuo Chú Chin Shih
                                      Lü Li Fu Hou
Classification B-147 史部-載記
                                           ba

Subject

References

Author 清   ching,
        喜, 邵懿辰 月, Shiao I-Chên

Edition 半巖廬所書書本 Pan-Yen-Lu-So edition
        明萬歷二十六年戊戌
        大字,   large Big characters

Index
        none

Bound in
        1 t'ê 1 t'ao

Remarks

....

Accession No. 1831   Index No. 085-nkjc

Title 濟寧縣志、(四卷)濟寧直隸州續志、(二十四卷)
Chi Ning Hsien Chih (Ssŭ Chüan), Chi Ning Chih Li Chou Hsü Chih (Êrh Shih Ssu Chüan)

Classification B194

Subject

References

Author 民國 潘守廉等纂修(重修)
Compiled by Republic, Pán Shou-Lien
Edition 民國十六年刊
Block engraving in the 16 year of the Republic

Index

Bound in 2 Tao 16 Tsê

Remarks

81

Accession No. *1832*   Index No. *163- Kz1b*

Title 郭文簡公文集 *Kuo Wên Chien Kung Wên Chi*

Classification *D-43*

Subject

References

Author 清 董襄編 明郭朴作品
Edited by Ching, Tung Hsiang (Ming, Kuo Pó's original copy)
Edition 康熙 甲寅年 思齊軒藏板
Block preserved Ssŭ-Chi-Hsüan

Index

Bound in *1 Táo   1 Tsё*

Remarks

82

The University of Toronto Chinese Library

....

Accession No. 1833   Index No. 106. 弓d戈c

Title 白雲傳表 *Pai Yün Hsien Piao*

Classification B — 117 — 传記 — 冬籍

Subject *collected biographies*

References

Author 清, 元厥棠安著 *Ching, Yüan Yen Chung Shih*

Edition 私庵板, 白連紙, 奉版

Private family edition, "Pai-Lien" paper, wood block

Index *none*

Bound in 1 *thò*, 2 *t'cè*

Remarks

The University of Toronto Chinese Library

....

Accession No. 1834   Index No. 042-e7ce

3

Title 尚書約註 Shang Shu Yüeh Chu

Classification A-21

Subject

References

Author 清 任啟運纂 Compiled by Ching. Jen Chi - Yün

Edition 家藏版 Private family edition
毛邊紙 "Mao Pien" paper

Index

Bound in 1 Tao, 2 Tsê

Remarks

84

. . . .

Accession No. *1835*   Index No. *085-hmhe*

Title 漢學商兌 *Han Hsüeh Shang Tui*

Classification *C —13 儒學*

Subject *a general writing of "Han-Hsüeh"*

References

Author 清. 方東樹 述。 *gwen in Oral by* *Ching, Fang Tung-Shu*

Edition 浙江 書局刊本 先備庚子年刊, 綿連紙
Chê-Chiang Book Company, dated Kuang-Hsü "Kêng Tzŭ"/1900
"Mien-Lien" paper

Index *none*

Bound in / *t/go. 3 Chüan, 4 t'sê*

Remarks

85

The University of Toronto Chinese Library

....

Accession No. 1836   Index No. 120-0j8f

Title 續彙刻書目 Hsü Hui K'o Shu Mu

Classification B-342

Subject

References

Author 羅振玉 Lo chên Yü

Edition 庚子范氏雙魚室刊
Block-printing edition in Lien-Ping, Fan-shih,
Shuang'-yü-shih.

Index

Bound in

Remarks

86

The University of Toronto Chinese Library

· ·

Accession No. *1838*   Index No. *009-mmk*

Title   儀禮圖 *I Li Tu*

Classification   *A-51*

Subject

References

Author   清 張惠言述 *Given in Oral by*
                        Ching. Chang Hui-Yen

Edition   湖北崇文書局重刻本 *Hu-Pei, Chung-Wen book company re-engraving editions*

           同治九年刻   毛邊紙
Block engraving in the 9th year of "Tung Chih"
                    Mao Pien - paper
Index

Bound in   *1 Tao   6 chuan   3 Tsê*

Remarks

The University of Toronto Chinese Library

....

Accession No. 1839   Index No. 040-djg

Title 宋類詩畧 Sung So Yü

Classification C — 338 — 雜部 — 叢書

Subject a general collection of reprints of "Sung" Dynasty.

References

Author

Edition 原藝林 , 竹紙版
private, family edition, Bamboo paper

Index a general table of contents for 4 tie

Bound in 1 f'ao, 4 tie

Remarks

The University of Toronto Chinese Library
....

Accession No. *1841*   Index No. *128-g~88.*

Title 聖學入門 *Shêng Hsüeh Ju Mên*

Classification *C-13*

Subject

References

Author 清 彭世昌輯註 *Compiled & annotated by* ∧*Chïng, Pëng Shih-Châng*

Edition 光緒三年刊
Block-engraving in the 3rd year of Kuang-Hsii.

Index

Bound in *1 Tào 2 Tsè*

Remarks

The University of Toronto Chinese Library

. . . .

Accession No. 1842   Index No. 055 - a 3 b 3

Title 十二史言行畧 Nien Êrh Shih Yen Hsing Lüeh
書

Classification B — 12 已史

Subject

References

Compiled by
Author 清, 圆元旺, 輯 Ching. Kuo Yuan · Min

Edition 吳城版, 嘉慶 15 年刊, 竹紙
Private Family Home edition, dated chia ching 15/1810 . Bamboo paper

Index A detail table of contents for 42 Chüan

Bound in 1 tʻo, 42 Chüan, 16 tsê

Remarks

90

The University of Toronto Chinese Library
....

Accession No. 1843   Index No. 030-c h g l

Title 名賢畫像傳 Ming Hsien Hua Hsiang Chuan

Classification G 223 B-17

Subject

References

Author 王念典 撰歷代名家所畫良方聖賢像及傳 刊成册
Written by Wang Nien-Tien
Edition 民國三年　京師團庫鑄一杜印
          Ching Shih, Kuo-Chün-Chu-I Shê

Index

Bound in   1 Tʻao   2 Tsʻê

Remarks

Accession No. *1844*　　　　　　Index No. *011-7273*

Title 兩漢孱守 *Liang Han Mêng Shih*

Classification B~~伯西史~~ ?

　　　　　　　A - 156　小學 - 訓詁

Subject

References

Author 仁和 杭世駿 *郭鄉林*, *Jên-Ho, Hang Shih Chün* (郭纂)

Edition

Index *none*

Bound in *1 t'ao, 2 ts'ê, 5 chüan*

Remarks

The University of Toronto Chinese Library
....

Accession No. 1845   Index No. 040-lee3

Title 寫定尚書 Hsieh Ting Shang Shu

Classification A-21

Subject

References

Author 清 吳汝綸錄 Ching, Wu Ju-Lun

Edition 桐城吳氏家屬本 Tung-Chêng, Wu-Shih
光緒十八年印 線連紙
Printed in the 18 year of "Kuang Hsü" "Mien Lien" paper

Index

Bound in / Ts'ê

Remarks

93

The University of Toronto Chinese Library

....

Accession No. *1846*   Index No. *140-889 上3*

Title 苕經堂文集二編 *Ju Ching Táng Wên Chi Erh Pien*

Classification *D-43*

Subject

References

Author 唐文治著 *Táng . Wên-Chih*

Edition

Index

Bound in *1 Táo   4 Tsê*

Remarks

The University of Toronto Chinese Library

. . . .

Accession No. *1847*   Index No. *037-a b c d*

Title 天崇合刻 *Tien Chúng Ho Chao*

Classification *D — 73* 宗集一元 (*general collection — prose*)
                        Tsung-Chi — Wên

Subject *a general collection of prose with commentary about the Four Books*

References

Author 清, 祝桂雲輯, 光緒年刻, 竹紙
       Chíng, Chu Sung-Yün

Edition 兩儀堂,
        Liang-I-Tang, dated
                        ∧ *Kuang-Hsü period (1875 - 1908)*
        Bamboo paper

Index *a general table of contents for 6 the*

Bound in *1 too, 6 the*

Remarks

The University of Toronto Chinese Library

. . . .

Accession No. 1848   Index No. 046-3772

Title 山海經廣注 Shan Hai Ching Kuang Chu

Classification C-5∮o

Subject

References

Author 清 吳任臣注 Annotated by Ching. Wu Jen-Chen

Edition 乾隆卅一年刊 金閶書業堂藏板

Chin-Chang, Shu-Yeh-Tang block-preserved.

Index

Bound in 1 Tao 6 Tsê with pictures

Remarks

96

The University of Toronto Chinese Library

. . . .

Accession No. 1849   Index No. 030-b3l3

38

Title 古文舊書攷　附訪餘錄　*Ku Wên Chiu Shu Kao*
Fu Fang Yü Lu

Classification B-337

Subject

References

Author 日本島田翰著　*Tao Tien-Han (Japan)*

Edition 藝玉堂印　*Tsao-Yü-Tang printing*
白毛邊紙　*White "Mao Pien" paper*

Index

Bound in 1 *T'ao*　4 *Ts'e*

Remarks

48

Accession No. *1850*   Index No. *039- cm k g*

Title 字學匯海 *Wên Hsüeh Hui Hai*
                    Zi

Classification *A-161*

Subject

References

Author 清. 龍光甸等 *Ching, Lung Kuang-Hsün and others*

Edition 京都秀文齋刻版 *Ching Tu, & Hsiu-Wen-Chai*

光緒己丑出版 連史紙

Published in Kuang Hsü
"chi ch'ou" Period.   *"Lien-Shih" paper*

Index

Bound in *1 T'ao,   4 Ts'*

Remarks

The University of Toronto Chinese Library

. . . .

30
Accession No. 1851   Index No. 001-boc9

Title 三藩紀事本末 San San Fan Chi Shih Pên Mo

Classification B-32

Subject

References

Author 清 楊陸榮 編 edited by Ching, Yang Lu-Jung

Edition 家藏版 Private family edition
竹紙 Bamboo paper

Index

Bound in   4 Ts'a

Remarks

Accession No. 1852   Index No. 038-gjPi

Title 娱園叢刊 + 科 Yü Yüan Tsung Kán Shih Chung

Classification 叢書 C348

Subject collections of reprints

References

Author 清 沈守梅 Compiled by Chíng, Hsü Tsêng

Edition 自藏板, 印連紙
private family edition, "Mien-Lién" paper

Index a general table of contents for 4 時

Bound in 1 + 60, 4 時

Remarks

The University of Toronto Chinese Library

....

6

Accession No. 1854   Index No. 149-93 ²j

Title 說文篆韻譜 5 Shao Wên Chuan Yün Pʻu

Classification A-161

Subject

References

Author 清 徐鉉述 *Gwen in oral by* Chʻing, Hsü Hsüan

Edition 綿州李氏用吳縣馮氏本校 *Wu-Hsien, Fêng-Shih original copy*
Mien-Chou, Li-Shih revised

官堆紙 衣板 *wooden block.*
"Kuang Tui" paper

Index ‡

Bound in 1 Tao, 5 chuan, 2 Tsʻê

Remarks

101

The University of Toronto Chinese Library

. . . .

Accession No. 1855   Index No. 042-3mdd

Title 小 學 鈎 沈 Hsiao Hsüeh Kou Shên

Classification c-338

Subject

References

Author 清 任大椿纂輯 王念孫校 (嘉慶年)
Compiled by Ching, Jen Ta-Chün, Wang Nien-Sun (revised)
Edition 光緒丁亥年重刊 書華閣藏板
Reprinted in Kuang Hsü "Ting-Hai" Shu-Hua-Ko block preserved.

Index

Bound in 1 Táo 2 Ts`è

Remarks

102

The University of Toronto Chinese Library

. . . .

4

Accession No. 1856   Index No. 005-ag k

Title 九經圖 Chiu Ching Tu

Classification A-137

Subject

References

Author 清 楊魁植 編輯 edited & compiled by
Ching, Yang Kui-Chih

Edition 翁園藏版 Hsi-Yüan block preserved.
乾隆壬辰年刻 連史紙 "Lien Shih" paper

Index Block engraving in ch'ien Lung "Jen ch'en" period.

Bound in 1 Tao, 10 Tsê

Remarks

The University of Toronto Chinese Library

. . . .

12

Accession No. 1857   Index No. 024-3b9k

Title 十三經摹本 *Shih San Ching Mu Pên*

Classification A-161

Subject

References

Author 清 彭玉雯纂, *Compiled by Ch'ing, Pêng Yü-Wên*

Edition 彭氏刊本 *Pêng-shih block print edition.*

綿連紙 夾板 ~~and~~ *wooden block.*

"Mien Lien" paper

Index

Bound in 1 *T'ao*   8 *Ts'ê*

Remarks

The University of Toronto Chinese Library

. . . .

96

Accession No. 1858   Index No. 036-b3d

Title 外制集 Wai Chih Chi

Classification B-117

Subject

References

Author 明 高拱 著 Ming, Kao Kung

Edition 高氏重刻本 Kao-Shih reprinted edition.
康熙己巳年重刊 毛邊紙
"Mao Pien" paper

Index

Bound in 1 Tao, 2 Ts'e

Remarks

The University of Toronto Chinese Library

. . . .

Accession No. 1859   Index No. 075-eЛ83

Title 柏堂遺書 Po Táng I Shu

Classification c-338

Subject

References

Author 清 方宗誠著 Chíng, Fang Tsung-Chéng

Edition 光緒三年刊開雕 志學堂家藏板
Chih-Hsüeh-Táng private family edition

Index

Bound in 8 Táo   48 Tsè

Remarks

The University of Toronto Chinese Library

. . . .

Accession No.   1860   Index No. 075-8887

Title   槐廬叢書 Huai Lu Tsung Shu

Classification   C-338

Subject

References

Author   清 朱懋之輯訂 *Compiled o bounded by* Ching, Chu Mao-Chih

Edition   光緒十四年刊   朱氏家塾藏板
Block-engraving in the   Chu-Shih Chia Shu private school edition
14th year of Kuang Hsü.
Index

Bound in   10 Táo   80 Tsʻë

Remarks

The University of Toronto Chinese Library

....

Accession No. 1862   Index No. 181-lgdd

Title 顧亭林先生遺書十種 *Ku Ting Lin Hsien Shêng I Shu Shih Chung*

Classification

Subject

References

Author 清 顧亭林著 *Ching, Ku Ting-Lin*

Edition 蓬瀛閣校刊   掃葉山房印
Collated ed. by Fêng-Ying-Ko   *Sao Yeh Shan Fang printing*

Index

Bound in 2 *Táo*   16 *Tsê*

Remarks

The University of Toronto Chinese Library

. . . .

Accession No. 1863   Index No. 085·738ᶜ

Title 津門雜記 *Chin Mên Tsa Chi*

Classification 0-217

Subject

References

Author 張燾輯 *Compiled by Chang Tao*

Edition 光緒十年甲申秋月新刻

Index

Bound in 1 Tao, 3 Ts'ê, 3 chuan (上,中,下)

Remarks

The University of Toronto Chinese Library

. . . .

Accession No. *1864*   Index No. *190-93*

Title 莊子 *Chuang Tzŭ*

Classification 乙一731 [子部]

Subject *Taoism — "*

References

Annotated by

Author 清, 王闓運 集註 *Ching, Wang Kai-yün*

Edition 王氏刊本, 毛元麻片[?] *Wang-Shih printed edition, "Yüan-Mao-Pien" paper*

Index *None*

Bound in *1 套, 2 冊*

Remarks

The University of Toronto Chinese Library

. . . . : . . . .

Accession No. 1865   Index No. 038/j d h h

Title 塊林漫錄   K'uei Ling Man Lu

Classification 已—308 群經—群經

Subject Miscellaneous writings + expositions

References

Author 清, 鄒式邦 撰 Written by ch'ing. chu shih TA. (5)

Edition 江蘇書局刊本, 光緒庚寅年刊, 綿連紙
Chiang-Su Book Company edition. dated Kuang-Hsü "Kêng-Yin"
/1890.
"Mien-Lien" paper

Index A general table of contents for 2 chüan

Bound in 1 t'ao, 2 ts'ê, 2 chüan

Remarks

111

The University of Toronto Chinese Library

· ·

Accession No. *1866*   Index No. *075-33ㄨ3*

Title 格言聯璧 *Ko Yen Lien Pi*

Classification *C—308 部首—部文*

Subject *miscellaneous writings of ethics & human behavior with commentary*

References

Author 清. 金蘭生著 *Ching, Chin Lan-Shêng*

Edition 仁济堂版. 光緒16年重刊, 毛四紙
Jên-Chi-Tang edition, dated Kuang-Hsü 16/1890, "Mao-Pien" paper

Index *a general table of contents for*

Bound in *1 t'ao, 2 ts'e*

Remarks

The University of Toronto Chinese Library

· ·

Accession No. *1867*   Index No. *085-7mi*

Title 洛學編 *Lo Hsüeh Pien*

Classification 乙—308 雜著一雜史

Subject *collection of*

References

Author 睢陽 湯文正公 *Compiled by* 撰 *Huai-Yang, Táng-Wèn-Chêng-Kung*

Edition 懷河堂藏本, 康熙 12年, 彩版, 黑三采一本 *Huai-Chien-Táng* preserved *edition, dated Káng-Hsi 12/1673, "Fên" paper, wood block*

Index *a general table of contents for 5 chüan*

Bound in *1 tào. 5 chüan, 1 tào*

Remarks

The University of Toronto Chinese Library

....

5

Accession No. 1869   Index No. 064-lamc

Title 撫本禮記 Fu Pên Li chi

Classification A-56

Subject

References

Author 清鄭康成註 *Annotated by* Ch'ing, Chêng Kang-Chêng

Edition 張敦仁仿宋本刻   崇文書局重彫 Chang Tun-Jen
同治九年刻   綿連紙 Chung Wên book company
"Mien Lien" paper

Index Detailed table of Content of 20 chuan.

Bound in 1 Tao, 8 本冊

Remarks

The University of Toronto Chinese Library

. . . .

Accession No. *1871*   Index No. *072-dci*

Title 易知編 *I Chih Pien*

Classification 七—308 雜文

Subject *Miscellaneous writings of ethics & human behavior*

References

Author 李廷謨 編輯 *edited & compiled by* *Li Ting-Lin*

Edition 蘇州織造署藏板 嘉慶辛刻, 己巳版, 木版
Su-Chou Chih-Tsao-Shu edition, preserved, dated Chia-Ching period,
"Mao-Pien" paper, wood block

Index *a general table of contents for 2 Chüan*

Bound in *1 t'ao, 2 chüan, 2 ts'e*

Remarks

Accession No. 1872   Index No. 030-bbji

Title 古今謠諺 Ku Chin Yao Yen

Classification C-510

Subject

References

Author 明 楊慎纂   清 史夢蘭補註
Compiled by Ming, Yang Shên; Ching, Shih Mêng-Lan (commentary)
Edition 清 同治癸酉年刊   止園莊板
Block engraving in Ching, Tung Chih   Chih-Yüan-Chuang
        "Kuei Yu" Period.

Index

Bound in   1 T'ao   4 Ts'ê

Remarks

The University of Toronto Chinese Library

. . . .

Accession No. 13 1873   Index No. 053-入iii

Title 廣韻新編 Kuang Yün Hsin Pien

Classification A-166

Subject

References

Author 勉學堂編, edited by Mien Hsüeh-Táng

Edition 家藏版 Private family edition
康熙年刻 榜紙
Block engraving in "Kang-Hsi" Period. "Pang" paper

Index

Bound in 1 Ts'ǎ

Remarks

. . . .

Accession No. *1874*　　　　　Index No. *075-jcng*

Title 榕村藏秘稿 *Jung Tsun Tsang Kao*

Classification *C-13*

Subject

References

Author 安溪先生榕村藏稿 ~~*Preserved draft*~~ 略由 *An Hsi Hsien Shêng Jung Tsun Tsáng Kao*

Edition

Index

Bound in *1 Táo　3 Tsʻé*

Remarks

The University of Toronto Chinese Library

· ·

Accession No. *1875*   Index No. *031-dbgdf*

Title 四庫全書表文箋釋 *Ssŭ Kù Chüan Shu Piao Wên Chien Shih*

Classification *B—342* 目錄一經籍

Subject *catalogues of ~~books~~ writings in general*

References

Author 清 林鶴年纂 *Compiled by Chʻing, Lin Ho-Nien*

Edition 求是齋刊，宣統年刻，白毛邊紙
Chiu-Shu-Chai edition, dated Hsüan-Tung period (1909-1911), white "Mao-Pien" paper

Index *separate table of contents for each chüan*

Bound in *1 t/ao, 4 chüan -, 4 tsê*

Remarks

The University of Toronto Chinese Library

. . . .

Accession No. 1876　　　　Index No. 037-akai

Title 天棠白齋 Tien Chüng Pai Pien

Classification D—73 詞各集—文

Subject Selections from the prose writings of ancient
scholars, with commentary

References

Author 清, 吳懋政選輯 Selected & Compiled by Ching, Wu Mao-Chêng

Edition 經國書局重刊, 光緒辛卯仲秋
Ching Kuo Book Company edition, dated Kuang-Hsü "Hsin-Mao"
autumn
1891

Index a general table of contents for 4 Chüan—

Bound in / t'ao, 4 Chüan, 4 tsê

Remarks

Accession No. *1877*   Index No. *031-6c 美九*

Title 四字類賦 *Ssŭ Tzŭ Lei Fu*

Classification *c-348*

Subject

References

Author 清 張師載 撰 *Written by* *Ching. Chang Shih-Tsai*

Edition 道光乙酉年新鐫   樂彼園藏版

Lo-Pi-Yüan Preserved edition.

Index

Bound in   *1 Táo   4 Tsè*

Remarks

The University of Toronto Chinese Library

. . . .

6

Accession No. *1878*   Index No. *031-b7&g*

Title 四書成語集對 *Ssŭ Shu Chéng Yü Chi Tuéi*

Classification *A-131*

Subject

References

Author 清揭裕忱輯 *Compiled by*
Chíng, Chieh Yü-Chén

Edition 昭然堂藏版 *Chao-Jan Táng block preserved.*

光緒癸巳年刊 毛邊紙

Block engraving in Kuang Hsü   *"Mao Pien" paper*

Index   *"Kuei chi" period.*

Bound in *1 Tao, 2 Ts'ê*

Remarks

122

The University of Toronto Chinese Library

....

Accession No. 1879   Index No. 125.333

Title 老解老 (老子道德經) Lao Chieh Lao (Lao Tzŭ Tao Tê Ching)

Classification C-731

Subject

References

Author 蔡廷幹編 edited by Tsai Ting-Kan

Edition 民國十一年刊 Block engraving in the 11th year of the Republic.

Index

Bound in   1 Tao   1 Tsʻe

Remarks

The University of Toronto Chinese Library

· ·

Accession No. 1880   Index No. 173-dd bz

Title 雲間三子合稿 Yün Chien San Tzŭ Ho Kao

Classification D-38

Subject

References

Author 雲間三子 (陳子龍、李雯、宋徵輿) 著. 明清時人
Ming & Ching, Yün Chien San Tzu (Chên Tzŭ-Lung, Li Wên, Sung Chêng Yü)

Edition 民國三年 峭帆樓重校刻
Hsiao Fan Lou collated edition

Index

Bound in 1 Tao   2 Ts'ê

Remarks

124

. . . .

Accession No. *16* 1881   Index No. 077-1cic

Title 歷代循吏傳 *Li Tai Hsün Li Chuan*

Classification β-117

Subject

References

Author 清 朱軾輯 *Compiled by* *Ching, Chu Shih*

Edition 家藏版 綿連紙

Private family edition   *"Chia Lien" paper*

Index

Bound in 1 Tao, 6 Ts'ê   8 chuan

Remarks

125

The University of Toronto Chinese Library

. . . .

Accession No. 1882   Index No. 024-33C3

Title 十竹齋書畫譜 Shih Chu Chia Chai Shu Hua Pu

Classification C-223

Subject

References

Author 胡曰從摹古   張學畊重校
       Hu Yüeh-Tsung   Chang Hsüeh-Ching (revised)
Edition 清光緒己卯年邱瑞麟按原譜重刻

       Chiu Jui-Lin reprinted edition.

Index

Bound in 1 Tao   8 Tsê

Remarks

The University of Toronto Chinese Library

· ·

58

Accession No. 1883   Index No. 096. 3 id あ

Title 王陽明出身靖亂錄 Wang Yang Ming Chu Shen Ching Luan Lu

Classification β-107

Subject

References

Author 明 墨憨齋 編 ~ edited by Ming, Mo Kan-Chai

Edition 弘毅館列 Hung-I-Kuang
朝岡氏藏 高麗紙
Chao-Kang Shih Preserved. Korea Paper

Index

Bound in 1 Tao, 3 Ts'a   3 chuan

Remarks

127

Accession No. *1884*   Index No. *212-3 3 i l*

Title 龍文鞭影 *Lung Wên Pien Ying*

Classification ㄷ—328 雜家-雜纂

Subject

References

Author

Edition 尚絅堂居士纂 道光辛刻, 竹紙, 夫版
楙芝敬軒藏
*Shang-Ching-Chü edition, dated in Tao-Kuang period (1821-1850)
Bamboo paper, wood block*

Index *none*

Bound in *1 t'ao, 2 ch'üan, 2 t'ǎ*

Remarks

The University of Toronto Chinese Library

. . . .

Accession No. *1885*   Index No. *051-bgc*

Title 平叛记 *Ping, Pan Chi*

Classification *B—32* 纪事专集

Subject *a complete historical narrative of the* rebellion
in Sung "Chung — Cheng," 崇祯 Emperor
"Chung - chên"

References

Author 清 毛霦 编 edited by *Ching, Mao Pin*

Edition 原稿版，康熙年刊， 毛边纸
Private family edition, dated Kang-Hsi period (1875-1908)
"Mao-Pien" paper   1662-1722

Index *none*

Bound in *1 tào, 2 tsê*

Remarks

The University of Toronto Chinese Library

· ·

5

Accession No. 1886   Index No. 072-2178

Title 春秋律身錄 chún chiu Lü Shēn Lu

Classification A-101

Subject

References

Author 清 楊長年著 Chíng, Yang Chéng-Nien

Edition 家藏版 Private family edition
光緒年刻 粉紙
Black-engraving in Kuang Hsü "fēn" paper
Index   period.

Bound in 1 Tao, 22 chuan, 8 Tsè

Remarks

130

The University of Toronto Chinese Library

. . . .

Accession No. *1887*   Index No. *162·lebh*

Title 箋注六朝唐賦 *Hsüan Chu Liu Chảo Tảng Fu*

Classification *D — 118* 詞曲 — 詞箋

Subject *Commentaries on selected lyrics of* 六朝
Liu Chảo

References

Author 清, 馬傳庚選注, *Selected & Annotated by* *Ching, Ma Chüan-Kêng*

Edition 京都松林齋刊本 光緒丙子年刊, 綿連紙 *Ching-Tu, Sung-Lin-Chai edition, dated Kuang-Hsü "Ping Tzǔ"* /1876 *"Mien-Lien" paper*

Index *a general table of contents for 2 tse*

Bound in *1 tảo, 2 tsê*

Remarks

The University of Toronto Chinese Library

....

Accession No. *1888*   Index No. *173-g m d z*

Title 震澤先生別集 *Chên Tsê Hsien Shêng Pieh Chi*

Classification *D-43*

Subject

References

Author 王鏊輯, *Compiled by* *Wang Ao*

Edition 辛酉莫春鮮溪王氏重刊

Mo Chun
late spring.   Hsi Wang-Shih revised

Index

Bound in *1 Táo 2 Ts'ê*

Remarks

The University of Toronto Chinese Library

. . . .

Accession No. 1889   Index No. 140·0kjc

Title 藤陰雜記 Têng Yin Tsa Chi

Classification C-303

Subject

References

Author 清　吟梅居士戴璐著 Ching, & Yin Mei Chü Shih Tsai Lu

Edition 光緒三年重刊　　吳興會館藏版

Reprinted in the 3rd year of   Wu-Hsing Hui Kuang block preserved.
　　　　"Kuang Hsü"

Index

Bound in 1 Táo. 2 Ts'ä

Remarks

The University of Toronto Chinese Library

....

Accession No. 1891   Index No. 010-dng3

Title 先儒罪子言行錄 Hsien Ju Chao Tzŭ Yen Hsing Lu

Classification 七——13 儒家

Subject a collection of "Chao - Tzĕ"

References

Author 宋.趙復仁 { compiled & given in Oral by
      Sung, Chao Fu-gén   清.陳延的案已
                  Ching, Chén Ting-Chün

Edition 湖北崇文書局重刊, 同治九年刊, 佛連紙
      Hu-Pei Chúng-Wén book company, dated Túng-Chih 9/1870
      "Mien-Lien" paper, wood block

Index Separate table of contents for each chüan

Bound in 1 tŏi, 2 chüan, 2 tsĕ

Remarks

The University of Toronto Chinese Library

. . . .

Accession No. 37/1893   Index No. 085-1 pdz

Title 澄懷主人自訂年譜 Chêng Hui Chu Jen Tzŭ Ting Nien Pú

Classification B-107

Subject

References

Author 清 張廷玉 撰 ∧ Written by Chíng, Chang Ting-Yü

Edition 張校文重校刊 Chang Hsiao Wên revised
家藏版 毛邊紙
Private family edition. "Mao Pien" paper

Index

Bound in 1 Táo   6 chuan 2 Ts'ê

Remarks

The University of Toronto Chinese Library
. . . .

Accession No. *1894*   Index No. *075-38 校經*

Title 校經堂初集 *Hsiao Ching Táng Chú Chí*

Classification D-63 總集一詩文

Subject *general collections of poetry and prose of the graduate of "Hsiao-Ching-Táng".*

References

Author 清. 曹鴻勛手訂 *Chíng, Tsáo Hung-Hsün*

Edition 校經堂版 *Hsiao-Ching-Táng edition*
光緒乙酉 *dated Kuang-Hsü "I-Yu" 1885*
毛邊紙. 夾板 *"Mao-Pien" paper, wood block*

Index *1) Different tables of the names with simple ancestries of the graduates of "Hsiao-Ching-Táng" according to years.*
2) a general table of contents of 4 chüan.

Bound in *1 táo, 4 chüan, 2 tsé.*

Remarks

The University of Toronto Chinese Library

. . . .

Accession No. *1895*   Index No. *159.* 𝓉𝒹𝓁

Title 輟耕錄. *Chʻo Kêng Lu*

Classification *C — 308* 部的 一 類文

Subject

References

Author 明, 陶宗儀 撰 *Written by*, *Ming, Tʻao Tsung-I*

Edition 井邑陶九泉之芸刊 筆宏紙 善本
光緒乙酉年上海福瀛書局重刊藏本
Wu-Chin, Tʻao-Shih, Chin-Yüan-Pên edition. "Tan-Hsüan" paper,
dated Kuang-Hsü "I-Yu" 1885. Shanghai Fu-Yin Book Company edition.

Index *a general table of contents for 30 Chüan*

Bound in *1 tʻao, 30 Chüan, 10 tsʻê*

Remarks

Accession No. *1896*   Index No. *149-0bzz*

Title 讀史管見 *Tu Shih Kuan Chien*

Classification *B-367*

Subject

References

Author 清　蘇文庵著 (道光二十九年) *Ching, Su Wên An*

Edition 光緒年刊　　本宅藏板

Blok engraving in   Pêng Chai block preserved.
"Kuang Hsü" period.

Index

Bound in   *1 Táo   4 Ts'ǔ*

Remarks

The University of Toronto Chinese Library

. . . .

18

Accession No. 1897   Index No. 030-bb

Title 史外 Shih Wai

Classification B-117

Subject

References

Author 清 汪有典著 Ching, Wang Yu-Tien

Edition 家藏版 朱檉之藏   Chu Shêng-Chih
        Private family ed.
        光緒丁丑年刻   毛太紙
        block engraving in Kuang Hsü   "Mao Tai" paper
Index   "Ting ch'ou"

Bound in 1 Tao, 8 Ts'è   8 chüan

Remarks

139

The University of Toronto Chinese Library

....

Accession No. *1898*   Index No. *140-giuc*

Title 莫愁湖志、 *Mo Chou Hu Chih*

Classification *B-207*

Subject

References

Author 馬士圖 輯著。 *Compiled by Ma Shih-Tú*

Edition 光緒壬午四月重鎸

Index

Bound in *1 Tao, 2 Tsʻe*

Remarks

The University of Toronto Chinese Library

· ·

Accession No. *1899*   Index No. *008-dggd*

Title 赤園亭全集 *I Yüan Ting Chüan Chi*

Classification *D-33*

Subject

References

Author 清 孟超然撰 *Written by Ch'ing, Mêng chāo-jan*

Edition 嘉慶二十年刊
block engraving in the 20th year of Chiā-Ch'ing.

Index

Bound in *1 T'áo   20 Ts'ê*

Remarks

The University of Toronto Chinese Library

．．．．．．．．．．．．．．．．．．．．．．．

23

Accession No. 1900   Index No. 024-ga bj

Title 十七史蒙求 附李氏蒙求補注六卷
      Shih Chi Shih Mêng Chiu
Classification B-137 *Fu Li Shih Mêng Chiu Chu Liu Chüan*

Subject

References

Author 清 王逢原著 *Ching, Wang Fêng-Yüan*

Edition 文奎堂版 *Wên Kui-Táng*
       道光年刻 白紙
Block engraveng in "Tao Kuang" period. "white paper

Index

Bound in 1 Tao   16 chuan   6 Ts'è

Remarks

The University of Toronto Chinese Library

. . . .

Accession No. 1901   Index No. 041-7ekg

Title 封神演義 fêng shên yen I

Classification C-368

Subject

References

Author 鍾伯敬批評 Commented & Annotated by Chung Po-Ching

Edition 掃葉山房刊 Sao-Yeh-Shan-Fang block-engraving.

Index

Bound in 2 Téo   20 Ts'é

Remarks

The University of Toronto Chinese Library
. . . .

Accession No. *1902*   Index No. *037-aezd*

Title 太祖高皇帝聖訓 *Tái Tsu Kao Huang Ti Shêng Hsün*

Classification *B—67* 治令奏清一治令

Subject *Imperial Edicts etc. of Emperor Tai-Chu*

References

Author 清太祖 *Ching Tai-Tsu Emperor*

Edition 殿版. 開化紙, 乾隆四年十二月
Palace edition, "Kai-Hua" paper, made in, dated Chien-Lung 4. 12th month
/ *1739*

Index *A general table of contents for 4 Chüan*

Bound in / *Táo, 4 Chüan, 4 Tsè*

Remarks

144

The University of Toronto Chinese Library

....

Accession No. *1903*   Index No. *075-6363*

Title 朱子古文 *Chu Tzŭ Ku Wên*

Classification *D——73* 張裳文

Subject *a general collection of prose with commentaries*

References

Author 清，周大璋偹大, *edited by* *Ching, Chou Ta-Chang*

Edition 寶研齋此宅藏版 道光乙未年刻 貴州棉紙
Pao-Yen-Chai Hua-Chai *block preserved* *edition, dated Tao-Kuang "I-Wei"* */1835*
"Kuei-Chou Mien" paper

Index *a general table of contents for 6 Chüan*

Bound in *1 Tao, 6 Chüan, 6 Tsè*

Remarks

145

The University of Toronto Chinese Library

. . . .

28

Accession No. 1404   Index No. 061-dzbc

Title (廿) 一史約編 Nien I Shih Yüeh Pien
念

Classification β-137

Subject

References

Author 清 鄭元慶述 Given in Oral by
        ∧Ching, Chêng Yüan-Ching

Edition 江左書臨林藏版 Chiang-Tsuo-Shu-Lin block preserved ed.
         竹紙 Bamboo paper

Index

Bound in 1 T'ao   8 chuan   8 Ts'ê

Remarks

146

The University of Toronto Chinese Library

· ·

Accession No. 1905~   Index No. 085-ngec

Title 濟南府志, Chi Nan Fu Chih

Classification β 194

Subject

References

Author 清　鐘祥　王鎮荤重修 Ching, Chung Hsiang; Wang Chên and others revised

Edition 本衙藏板　道光二十年刊
庚子
Pêng Ya block preserved edition
Dated — Tao-Kuang "Kêng-Tzu" 20/1840

Index

Bound in 6 tao　40 Ts'ê　72 Chuan

Remarks

147

. . . .

Accession No. 1906   Index No. 120-cfgx

Title 紀元通攷 Chi yüan Tung Kao

Classification B-282

Subject

References

Author 葉維庚 Yeh Wei Kêng

Edition 道光八年鐫 鍾秀山房藏板
戊子
Ed.→Chung-Hsiu-Shan-fang block preserved edition

Dated — Tao-Kuang "Wu-Tzu" 8//1828

Index

Bound in 1 tao, 4 ts'è, 12 chüan

Remarks

The University of Toronto Chinese Library
. . . .

Accession No. 1907   Index No. 149-ㄌ3ㄇ7

Title 郝子隨筆節鈔 Kó Tzǔ Sui Pi Chieh Cháo

Classification C—13 儒法

Subject A collection of ancient scholars' writings of
儒教

References

Author 清, 張朱梁輯 Compiled by Ching, Chang Yu-Chü

Edition 家藏版, 毛邊紙
Private family edition, "Mao-Tái" paper

Index A general table of content for 6 chüan

Bound in 1 táo, 6 chüan, 4 tsê, & continue 1 chüan

Remarks

149

The University of Toronto Chinese Library
....

Accession No. *1908*   Index No. *072-ecp8*

Title 昭代叢書丙集 *Chao Tai Tsung Shu Ping Chi*

Classification *C-338*

Subject

References

Author 清　張潮　張漸　同輯 *Compiled by Ching. Chang Chao and Chang Chien*

Edition 康熙四十二年刊　癸未　詒清堂藏板 *I-Ching-Tang block preserved ed.*
Dated — Kang-Hsi "Kuei-Wei" 42/1703

Index

Bound in *1 t'ao　8 ts'è*

Remarks

The University of Toronto Chinese Library

· ·

Accession No. *35* *1909*   Index No. *075-d h b g*

Title 東國史略 *Tung Kuo Shih Lüeh*

Classification *B-52*

Subject

References

Author

Edition 景蘇園校刊 *Ching-Su Yüan rivised ed. collated edition*

光緒癸巳年刊　綿連紙　夾板

Index *"Mien Lien" paper Wooden block*
Dated — Kuang-Hsü "Kuei-Ssu" 19/1893

Bound in *1 t'áo   6 chuan   2 ts'è*

Remarks

The University of Toronto Chinese Library

....

Accession No. *1910*   Index No. *030-bbgd*

Title 古今事物考 *Ku Chin Shih Wu Kao*

Classification *C-348*

Subject

References

Author 王三聘 輯 *Compiled by* *Wang San-Pin*

Edition

Index

Bound in *1 t'ao 4 ts'e*

Remarks

152

The University of Toronto Chinese Library

. . . .

Accession No. *1911*   Index No. *036-cih3*

Title 多藏堂詩集 *To Sui Táng Shih Chi*

Classification *D-38*

Subject

References

Author 清 成書萼 *Chíng, Chéng Shu*

Edition

Index

Bound in *1 táo   4 tsê*

Remarks

5'5'

Accession No. 1912   Index No. 060-光e光c

Title 御定萬年書 Yü Ting Wan Nien Shu

Classification B-157

Subject

References

Author

Edition 連史紙 "Lien Shih" paper

Index

Bound in 1 t'ao. 2 ts'e

Remarks

154

Accession No. *1913*   Index No. *120·C3*

Title 約書 *Yüeh Shu*

Classification *C-308* 雜家 — 雜文 *(Miscellaneous Writing)*
                      Tsa Chia Tsa Wen

Subject *miscellaneous writing of* "信義"
                                    Hsin I

References

Author 清, 謝階樹撰, *Written by* *Ch'ing, Hsieh Chieh-Shu*

Edition 志素堂, 亘光寺
Private family Home edition, dated Tao-Kuang period (1821-1850)

Index *a general table of contents for 12 chüan*

Bound in *1 t'ao, 4 tse, 12 chüan*

Remarks

The University of Toronto Chinese Library
. . . .

Accession No. 1914   Index No. 072-2g2g

Title 景教碑文紀事考証 Ching Chiao Pei Wên Chi Shih Kao Chêng

Classification C-985

Subject

References

Author 清 楊榮鋕著 Ch'ing, Yang Jung-Chih

Edition 光緒二十未年刊
       Dated — Kuang-Hsü "I-Wei" 21/1895 block-engraving

Index

Bound in 1 t'ao   3 ts'e

Remarks

156

The University of Toronto Chinese Library
....

Accession No. 1916   Index No. 037-3义33

Title 大清律例增修统纂集成 Ta Chìng Lü Li Tsêng Hsiu Túng
                               Tsuan Chi Chêng

Classification β-302

Subject

References

Author 世祖章皇帝御製 made by Shih Tsu Chang Emperor Hoang Ti

Edition 蓬武林清來堂吳氏原本增修 Revised Tsan Wu Lin. Chìng Lai-Táng Wu-Shih
                                    Original copy
        光绪二十年印
        Dated — Knong-Hsü "Chia-Wu" 20/1894

Index

Bound in 4 tao, 24 ts'e

Remarks

157

The University of Toronto Chinese Library

· ·

Accession No. 1917   Index No. 049-a-zai

Title 巴山七种 Pa Shan Chi Chung

Classification 書号 C 308

Subject collection of reprints in seven kinds
冠服, 治平要术 死亡, 诗存, 衡言, 文存
举误. Kuan Fu, Chih Ping Yao Shu, Fang Yen, Shih Tsun,
Hêng Yen, Wên Tsun, Pi Tan,

References

Author 清王修槐 Written by Ching, Wang Kân

Edition 光裕堂刊 同治年刊, 竹纸
Kuang-Yü-Tâng block engraving edition, dated Tûng-Chih period (1862-1874)
Bamboo Paper

Index a table of contents only for the first tsê

Bound in 1 tâo, 8 t'sê, 共七种
7 types

Remarks·

158

The University of Toronto Chinese Library
....

Accession No. 1918   Index No. 005-2233

Title 乾坤大畧 Chien Kun Ta Yin

Classification 己一308 雜著 一 雜文

Subject miscellaneous writings of poetry

References

Author 清, 劉鶴壽輯 Compiled by Ching, Liu Chang-chu

Edition 范氏家藏版 同治十三年刻, 竹紙
Fan-Shih private family home edition, dated Tung-Chih 13/1874
Bamboo paper

Index a general table of contents for 8 tse

Bound in 1 t'ao, 8 tse

Remarks

The University of Toronto Chinese Library

. . . .

3

Accession No. *1919*   Index No. *076. Leiz*

Title 欽定篆文四書 *Chin Ting Chuan Wên Ssu Shu*

Classification *A-131*

Subject

References

Author

Edition 古今圖書局仿原本影印 *Ku Chin Tú Shu Chü Photo - lithographic ed.*
廣益書局   連史紙 *Lien Shih° paper*
Kaang I· Shu Chü

Index

Bound in *1 tao,   6 tsê*

Remarks

The University of Toronto Chinese Library

· ·

Accession No. *1920*   Index No. *109-dhgo*

Title 盾鼻餘瀋 *Tun Pi yü shên*

Classification *C - 328* 雜家 — 雜纂

Subject

References

Author 柳葆元昌策謙錄刊

Edition *Liu Pao-yüan I tsê Chien Lu Copied from block-print edition.*
家藏版 *Private family* *Home edition*
光緒七年刻竹紙 *dated Kuang-Hsü 7/1881. Bamboo paper*
block engraving edition.

Index

Bound in
1 tào, 1 tsê

Remarks

The University of Toronto Chinese Library
....

Accession No. *1922*   Index No. *128·ecc8*

<u>Title</u> 聊齋志異新評 *Liao Chai Chih I Hsin Ping*

<u>Classification</u> *c-368*

<u>Subject</u>

<u>References</u>

<u>Author</u> 蒲松齡著   王士正評   但明倫新評
Pú Sung-Ling; Wang Shih-Chêng and Tan Ming-Lung (reviews)
<u>Edition</u> 清光緒丁丑年開雕 兩餘堂藏板 *(commentaries)*
Liang-Yü Táng
Dated — Ching, Kuang — Hsü "Ting-Chóu" 3/1877
<u>Index</u>

<u>Bound in</u> *2 t'áo*   *16 ts'ó*

<u>Remarks</u>

The University of Toronto Chinese Library

．．．．．．．．．．．．．．．．．．．．．．．．

Accession No. 1923   Index No. 030-9 edb

Title 唐丞相曲江張文獻公集 Táng Cheng Hsiang Chu

Classification △   Chiang Chang Wen Hsien Kung Chi

Subject

References

Author 唐張九齡撰 Written by Tang, Chang Chiu Ling

Edition 曲江裔孫張曉如重刊明本

~~中華書局~~ Chang Hsiao & Ju repirinted Ming edition

Index

Bound in 十二卷六冊 12 Chuan 6 Tsé

Remarks 光緒壬辰年重刊 Reprinted ed. in Kuang Hsü "Jen chen" period

錦連紙 Mien-Lien Paper

木板 Wooden block.

163

The University of Toronto Chinese Library

· ·

Accession No. *1924*   Index No. *064-ᴸℓpⁱ*

Title 掌故叢編 *Chang Ku Tsung Pien*

Classification *B-367*

Subject

References

Author 清、薛福成 葦兩作掌故共七種 *Ch'ing, Hsüeh Fu-Ch'êng and others*
       ~~Ching,~~

Edition 光緒辛丑年　掃葉山房石印
        Sao-Yeh-Shan-Fang lithographic
        Dated — Kuang-Hsü "Hsin-Chou" 27/1901

Index

Bound in *2 t'ao   14 ts'*

Remarks

164

The University of Toronto Chinese Library

. . . .

Accession No. *1945*   Index No. *186-382*

Title 香祖筆記 *Hsiang Tzu Pi Chi*

Classification *E-308* 雜文

Subject *Miscellaneous writings*

References

Author 清, 王士正著 *Ching, Wang Shih-Chêng*

Edition 申報館印, 竹紙, 排印 *Shên-Pao-Kuan printed, Bamboo paper, Type-setting edition*

Index *none*

Bound in *1 tʻao, 12 chüan, 4 tsê*

Remarks

The University of Toronto Chinese Library

. . . .

Accession No. /9x6   Index No. 060-hhmu

Title 御製避暑山莊詩 Yü Chih Pi Shu Shan Chuang Shih

Classification D—38 別集一詩

Subject an individual collection of poetry; with commentary

References

Author 清聖祖製祖仁至帝御製

made by ching, Huang Tzu Shêng Tzŭ Jên Huang Ti

Edition 啟版, 乾隆辛酉年 杉版

Palace edition, dated chien lung "Hsin-Yu" /1741

powder for paper

Index a general table of contents for 2 tse

Bound in 1 tao, 2 tse

Remarks

166

26

Accession No. 1927   Index No. 162-inzh

Tao Tsang Mu Lu Hsiang Chu
Fu Hsü Tao Tsang Mu Lu

Title 道藏目錄詳註 附續道藏目錄

Classification B-342

Subject

References

Author 明 道士白雲齋霽 撰 ∧ *Written by* Ming (Tao-Shih) Pai Yün-Chi

Edition 退耕堂景印文津閣四庫全書本 Tui Kêng Tang Ching Yin Wên Ching Ko
綿連紙 *Mien Lien paper* Ssŭ Kü Chüan Shu Pên

Index

Bound in 1 táo   4 chuan   4 tsʻᵉ

Remarks

The University of Toronto Chinese Library
. . . .

Accession No. 1929   Index No. 069-1ee3

Title 新政真詮 Hsin Chêng Chen Chüan

Classification β-277

Subject

References

Author 南海何啟沃生 (Nan-Hai) Ho Chi Wo Shêng
三水胡禮垣翼南 (San-Shui) Hu Li Yüan I Nan

Edition 清光緒辛丑重刊版
格致新報館印
Ko-Chih-Hsin Pao Kuang

Index Dated — Ching, Kuang-Hsü "Hsin-Ch'ou" 27/1901
re-printed edition.

Bound in 1 tao, 8 ts'ê

Remarks

168

Accession No. *1930 - 3*   Index No. *053 · lg 赤*

Title 廣事類賦 *Kuang Shih Lei fu*

Classification *L - 348*

Subject

References

Author 清華希閔著 *Ching, Hua Hsi-Min*

Edition 康熙三十八年   芥子園藏版
                己卯
                Chieh-Tzŭ-Yüan block preserved edition
         Dated — Kang-Hsi "Chi-Mao" 38/1699

Index

Bound in *1 t'ao 8 ts'e*

Remarks

The University of Toronto Chinese Library

....

Accession No. 1931   Index No. 106-d h t z

Title 皇朝駢文類苑 Huang Ch'ao P'ien Wen Lei Yüan

Classification △

Subject

References

Author 清姚燮選 Selected by Ch'ing, Yao Hsieh

Edition 掃葉山房藏版 Sao Yeh Shan Fang blocks preserved edition.

Index

Bound in 十五卷二十四冊 15 Chüan, 24 Ts'e

Remarks 光緒年刊 Block-engraving in Kuang Hsü period
         粉連紙 Powder-like cotton paper.
         夾紙 Wooden block

170

The University of Toronto Chinese Library

....

Accession No. *1932*   Index No. *007-b3c9*

Title 五十名家尺札 *Wu Shih Ming Chia Shu Tsa*

Classification *D-73* 總集・文

Subject *a general collection of 50 well-known writings writers' personal letters*.

References

Author

Edition 潛園摹刻

Chien-Yüan printed block-engraving edition

Index *None*

Bound in *1760, 3 the*

Remarks

012

The University of Toronto Chinese Library
. . . .

Accession No. 1933   Index No. 019-rc88

Title 勸戒詩話 Chüan Chieh Shih Hua

Classification D—63 總集—詩文

Subject a general collection of poetry & prose

References

Author 清，黃坤元編輯 edited & compiled by Ching, Huang Kun-Yüan

Edition 翼經堂藏版，文藝榮木刻刊，綿連紙
I-Ching-Tang edition, block preserved dated Kuang-Hsü "Kuei-Wei" 1883
"Mien-Lien" paper

Index none

Bound in 1 t'ao, 8 chüan, 4 ts'é

Remarks

The University of Toronto Chinese Library

....

Accession No. *1934*   Index No. *106-dh93*

Title 皇清經解縮板編目 *Huang Ching Ching Chieh So Pan Pien Mu*

Classification 考書 *A-137*

Subject *catalogue of the commentaries of classics*

References

Author 清, 王先謙編輯 *edited & compiled by Ching, Wang Hsien-Chien*

Edition 江陰南菁書院 書局刊年, 共209种, 光緒
十五年刋, 毛巳紙
Chiang-Yin Nan-Ching-Shu Yüan Book Company edition, 209 Types, dated Kuang-Hsü 15/1889, "Mao-Pien" paper

Index *a general table of contents for 2 t'se*

Bound in *1 t'ao, 2 t'se*

Remarks

The University of Toronto Chinese Library

. . . .

12

Accession No. *1935*   Index No. *072-dgge*

Title 易經通註 *I Ching Tûng Chu*

Classification *A-11*

Subject

References

Author 清 傅以漸撰 *Written by Ching, Fu I-Chien*

Edition 雖園校刊 巾箱本 *Sui Yüan revised, ~~Chin Hsiang~~ pocket- ed.*
光緒丙戌年刊 綿連紙

Index *Dated — Kuang-Hsü "Ping-Hsü" "Mien Lien" paper 12/1886 block engraved*

Bound in *1 t'ao   4 ts'e*

Remarks

The University of Toronto Chinese Library

. . . .

Accession No. *1936*　　　　　Index No. *030-9323*

Title 唐子僭書 *Táng Tzŭ Chien Shu*

Classification 乙 — *308* ~~雜家~~ — ~~雜文~~

Tsa Chia — *Tsa Wên*

Subject

References

Author 清. 唐甄著 *Ching, Táng Chên*

Edition 私藏版, ~~～世版~~ 竹紙紙

Private ~~house~~ *family edition*

　　　　Bamboo paper

Index *A general table of contents for a t'ae*

Bound in *1 t'ao,* *2* *t'aè*

Remarks

The University of Toronto Chinese Library

· ·

12

Accession No. 1937   Index No. 030-Ckim

Title 同聲韻學便覽 *T'ung Shêng Yün Hsüeh Pien Lan*

Classification A-166

Subject

References

Author 清 蒯德懋 編輯 *edited & compiled by Ch'ing, K'uai Tê-Mao.*

Edition 家藏版 *private — printed family edition*

光緒年刻   油光紙 *a kind of imported paper.*

Index *Dated — Knang-Hsü period 1875 → 1906 block engraving "Yu-Kuang" paper edition*

Bound in   4 chuan, 4 ts'ê

Remarks

Accession No. *1938*   Index No. *128-2CC8*

Title 聊齋志異新評 *Liao Chai chai chih I Hsin P'ing*

Classification 已 ~~375~~ ~~報告~~ ~~報告~~ 368. 小說家

Subject *Commentaries on the* 聊齋志異

　　　　　　　　　　　"Liao Chai Chih I"

References

Author 清, 蒲松齡撰 *Written by* *Ching, Pu Sung-Ling*

Edition 廣順 旦氏 刊, 石氏批評正文, 同治九年(己巳) 刊
　　　　　　　　　　　　　　　作閏識.
Kuang-Shun, Tan-Shih edition, commentaries printed in red,
dated Tung-Chih 9 "Chi Ssŭ" / 1869-1870

Index *"Mien-Lien" paper*

Bound in *2* 套, *16* chüan, *16* 冊

Remarks

. . . .

Accession No. *1939*   Index No. *106- a z m g*

Title 百川學海 *Po Ch'uan Hsüeh Hai*

Classification *c - 338*

Subject

References

Author 柳蓉村藏 *Liu Jung-Ts'un preserved.*

Edition "辛酉"年   上海博古齋印

Shanghai, Po-Ku-Chai printed.

Index

Bound in *4 t'ao   40 ts'e*

Remarks

The University of Toronto Chinese Library

....

Accession No. ~~7039~~ 1940   Index No. 149·C93

Title 泅事珠 Chi Shih Chu

Classification C—368

Subject ~~A Literary~~ 經史典故駢句

References

Written by
Author 清, 莊以謙撰, Ching. Chang I Chien

Edition 草木版, 上海掃葉山房校刻, 聚元堂藏板
光緒壬午年, 毛邊紙
          Shanghai, Sou-Yeh-Shan-Fang revised, Chü-Yüan-
Tang edition dated Kuang-Hsü "Jen Wu" 1882. "Hao-Pien" paper

Index a general table of contents for 10 chüan

Bound in 2 t'ao, 10 chüan, 10 ts'e

Remarks

179

The University of Toronto Chinese Library

. . . .

Accession No. *1941*   Index No. *044-a0cz*

Title 尺牘也園 *Chih Tu Ju Mien*

Classification *D—63* 總集一尺文

Subject *a general collection of all kind of letters in poetry or prose.*

References

Author 李鑽廷纂輯。 *Compiled by Li Tsan-Ting*

Edition 翠筠山房梓； 木板， 毛太紙
Ts'ai-Chün-Shan-Fang printed, wood block, "Mao-Tai" paper

Index *a general table of contents for 6 chüan*

Bound in *1 t̂o. 6 chüan 2 t̂ie*

Remarks *Originally bound in 6 t̂ie. Now bound in 2 t̂ie and bound in different order of the chüans which starts Chüan 6 → 5 → 1 → 2 → 3 → 4.*

180

The University of Toronto Chinese Library
....

Accession No. *1942*   Index No. *039.aP3*

Title   孔叢子 *Kúng Tsung Tzǔ*

Classification   *c-13* 儒家

Subject

References

Author   宋 宋咸註。 *Annotated by*
                    Sung, Sung Hsien

Edition   海昌 陳氏重刊 *Hai-Cháng, Chên-Shih revised edition*
          宋嘉祐本, 光緒年刻 *Sung Chia-Yu's copy*
          連史紙 *dated Kuang-Hsü period (1875-1908)*

Index   *"Lien-Shih" paper*
          A general table of contents for 7 chüan

Bound in   *1 t'ao   7 chüan   4 tsê*

Remarks

181

The University of Toronto Chinese Library

. . . .

Accession No. *1943*   Index No. *102-22ka*

Title 留荪盦人物攷残 *Liu Mao An Chih Tu Tsúng Tsáng*

Classification *D — 43*

Subject

References

Author 清,饒士竹纂   毛太纸   木版

Ching, Yen Shih-Chu   *"Mao Tái" paper, wood block*

Edition

Index

Bound in *1 táo   4 Chüan 2 tsê*

Remarks

The University of Toronto Chinese Library

· ·

Accession No. 1944   Index No. 149-03bc

Title 讀書分年日程 Tu Shu Fên Nien Jih Chêng

Classification B-289

Subject

References

Author 鄞 程端禮編 (Yin) Chêng Tuan-Li

Edition 光緒十八年文英閣刊
                     Wên-Yin-Ko published
Dated — Kuang-Hsü "Jên-Chên" 18/1892

Index

Bound in 1 tao, 2 ts'ê, 3 chuan

Remarks

The University of Toronto Chinese Library
....

20

Accession No. 1945   Index No. 060-hdlc

Title 御批歷代通鑑輯覽 Yü Pi Li Tai Tüng Chien Chi Lan

Classification B-22

Subject

References

Author 清康熙帝御批 傅恒等奉敕編纂
        Ching, Kang-Hsi Emperor, (commentary) Fu Hêng and others
Edition 鉛印本 Type-settinged

        洋紙 夾板 Wood-block
        imported Western paper

Index

Bound in 4 tao   120 chuan.   40 ts'ê

Remarks

The University of Toronto Chinese Library

....

Accession No. *1946*   Index No. *167-n1*

Title 鑑撮 四卷附讀史論略卷   *Chien Tso*
Ssŭ Chüan Fu Tu Shih Lun Lüeh I Chüan

Classification *B-367*

Subject

References

Author 清 曠敏本編 *edited by* *Ch'ing. Kuang Min-Pên*

Edition 同治年刊
Dated — Tùng-Chih period 1862-1874

Index

Bound in *1 t'ao   5 ts'ê*

Remarks

185

The University of Toronto Chinese Library

....

Accession No. *1947*   Index No. *120-2232e*

Title 繡像封神演義 *Hsiu Hsiang Fêng Shên Yen I*

Classification *C-308*

Subject

References

Author 鍾惺伯評釋 *Commented & explained by Chung Hsing-Po*

Edition 清光緒三十四年 集成圖書公司鑄印
         Chi-Chêng Tú Shu Kung Ssu
Dated — Ching, Kuang-Hsü "Wu-Sheng" 34/1908

Index

Bound in *1 t'áo   10 ts'ê*

Remarks

The University of Toronto Chinese Library

....

43

Accession No. 1949 A-B   Index No. 018-ghc

Title 前漢記, 後漢紀 *Chien Han Chi, Hou Han Chi*

Classification B-32

Subject

References

Author 漢 荀悅撰 (Written by) *Han, Hsün Yüeh*

Edition 嶺南學海堂刊本 *Ling-Nan, Hsüeh-Hai-Tang*

光緒丙子年刊 綿連紙

Index *Dated — Kuang-Hsü "Ping-Tzǔ" 2/1876* "Mien Lien" paper

Bound in 2 t'ao   62 chuan   14 ts'ê

Remarks

The University of Toronto Chinese Library

....

Accession No. *1950*　　　　Index No. *140-pdbj*

Title 蘇沈內翰良方 *Su Shên Nei Han Liang Fang*

Classification ⊂—*63* 醫药

Subject *a comprehensive writing of medicine*

References

Author 宋, 蘇軾, 沈匮集 括？ Collected by *Sung. Su Shih, Shên Ko*

Edition 計強賀氏仿知不足斋叢书校印
之藏丁酉手印, 絲連紙
*Wu-Chiang, Ho-Shih imitated "Chih-Pu-Tzu-Chai"
dated Kuang-Hsü "Ting-Yu"/1897　"Mien-Lien" paper*

Index *A general table of content for 10 Chüan.*

Bound in *1 t'ao, 10 chüan, 4 ts'ê*

Remarks

188

The University of Toronto Chinese Library

. . . .

Accession No. *1951*   Index No. *188-32jc*

Title 有聲畫社 *Ku Tung So Chi*

Classification 乙.—308 雜著 — 雜文

Subject *Miscellaneous writings*

References

Author 清, 鄧之誠輯 *Compiled by* *Ching, Teng Chih-Cheng*

Edition 明 崇禎七年, 鉛印 戊國 十五年, 洋白毛邊紙

Ming-Chai-Tsung-Shu-Pen, *Type-setting edition*
dated Republic 15/1926, *imported Western white "Mao-Pien" paper*

Index *none*

Bound in *1 t'ao, 8 chüan, 4 ts'ê*

Remarks

The University of Toronto Chinese Library

....

Accession No. 1952

3

Index No. 149-7ネクm
jc

Title 詩韻合璧 附 虚字韻藪 初學椒韻

Shih Yün Ho Pi
Fu Hsü Tzŭ Yün Sau
Ch'u Hsüeh Chien Yün

Classification A-166

Subject

References

Author

Edition 暢懷書屋校本 鴻寶齋印
光緒十七年印 重印 綿連紙

Ch'ang-Huai-Shu-Wu rivised
Hung-Pao-Chai

Index Dated — Kuang-Hsü "Hsin—Mao" 17/1891
"Mien Lien" paper

Bound in 1 t'ao 6 ts'ê

Remarks

190

The University of Toronto Chinese Library

. . . .

2

Accession No. 1953   Index No. 007-4736

Title 五經備旨 Wu Ching Pei Chih

Classification A-137

Subject

References

Author 清 鄒梧岡纂輯。 Compiled by Ching, Tsou Wu-Kang

Edition 大同書局石印 Ta-Tung book company type-setting ed.
光緒十三年印 油光紙 夾版 wooden block

Index Painting in The 13 Year of "Kuang" paper A kind of imported paper
Kuang Hsü

Bound in 1 tao, 12 tsê

Remarks

The University of Toronto Chinese Library

....

Accession No. *1954*   Index No. *067-37im*

Title 文昌遊戲 *Wên chang Yu Hsi*

Classification *D.— 43*

Subject

References

Author 武林、繆蓮仙輯 *Compiled by* *Wu-Lin, Miao Lien-Hsien*

Edition 光緒丙申孟夏上海積山書局石印
Dated Kuang-Hsü "Ping Shên," summer 1896
Lithographic edition
Shanghai, Chi-Shan Book Company,

Index 連史紙 *"Lien-Shih" paper*

Bound in *1 t'ao, 4 Pien 6 ts'ê*

Remarks

The University of Toronto Chinese Library

. . . .

Accession No. *1955*　　　　Index No. 031-*kheb*
　　　　　　　　　　　　　　　　　　　jdky

Title 國朝尚友錄 (A.) 二　　Kao Chao Shang Yu Lu (A)
　　　　尔雅圖古鉎 (B.) 二　　Enh Ya Tu Yin Chu (B)

Classification

　　　　(A) B-117　傳記-綫錄

Subject　　(B) C-258　譜錄

References　　　　　　edited & Compiled by,　　　　　(Yün Wu)
　　　　　　　　　^(A) Kao Yu, Li Pei-Fang (Shu Lan) and San Ting^

Author (A) 高邑　李佩芳淑蘭　錄　鼎韻武 編纂
　　　(B) 郭璞撰　　(B) Kúo Pu

Edition (A) 光緒壬寅夏五月　　上海南洋七日報館刊　杉連紙
　　　　(B) 光緒丁酉孟春　神記書莊石印　杉連紙

　　　(A) Dated Kuang-Hsü "Jên Yin" fifth month /1902
　　　　　　　　　　　　　　　　　　summer
Index　(B) Shanghai, Nan-Yang Chi-Jih Pao Kuan edition "Fên Lien" paper
　　　(B) Dated Kuang-Hsü "Ting Yü" spring /1897　　EA Shên-Chi-Shu Chuang
　　　　"Fên-Lien" paper　　　　　　　　　　　　Lithrographic edition

Bound in (A) 1 t'ao, 2 t'sc (8 chüan)

　　　(B) 1 t'ao, 2 t'sê

Remarks

193

The University of Toronto Chinese Library

. . . .

Accession No. *1956*   Index No. *181-頁夜*

Title 類腋 *Lei Yeh*

Classification *C-348*

Subject

References

Author 清 姚培謙集 *Collected by* *Ching, Yao Pei-chien*

Edition 乾隆壬戌年刊 綠蔭堂雕藏
Lü-Yin-Tang preserved.
Dated — Chien-Lung "Jêt-Hsü" 7/1742

Index

Bound in *4 t'ao 24 ts'u*

Remarks

The University of Toronto Chinese Library

· ·

Accession No. *1957*   Index No. *157-7ᵇ*

Title 路史   *Lu Shih*

Classification *B——般朝史*

Subject

References

Author 宋羅泌著   *Sung, Lo Pi*

Edition 校宋车縮印, 光緒甲午印, 綿連紙.
Imitated "Sung" edition, Dated Kuang-Hsü "Chia-Wu"/1894. "Mien-Lien" paper

Index *a general table of contents for 16 Chüan which divided into 5 sections & a table of contents for each section.*

Bound in *1 Tao, 16 Chüan, 6 Tsẻ*

Remarks

The University of Toronto Chinese Library

. . . .

Accession No. 1958   Index No. 031-b7bR

Title 四書古註九種羣義彙解 Ssŭ Shu Ku Chu Chiu Chung Chün I
Hui Chieh

Classification A—131

Subject

References

Author

Edition 石印袖珍本 Type-setting-pocket ed.
Hsi+ch+n
油光紙 夾板 Wood-block
"Yu Kuang" paper

Index

Bound in 2 t'ao   16 tsê

Remarks

The University of Toronto Chinese Library

. . . .

Accession No. 1959   Index No. 102-ngk

42

Title 田壽人傳 Chóu Jen Chüan

Classification B-117

Subject

References

Author 清 阮元撰 ∧ Ching, Juan J Yüan
                    Written by

Edition 海鹽常惺齋張氏重校刊袖珍本 Hai-Yen, Chang Hsin-Chai, Chang.
                                       Shih revised pocket ed.
       光緒年刻 連史紙 夾板 Wood-block

Index   Dated — Kuang-Hsü period 1895—1908
                   "Lien Shih" paper

Bound in 2 tao   46 chüan (附續傳六卷) 12 ts'e

Remarks

The University of Toronto Chinese Library
....

Accession No. *1960*   Index No. *111-cjca*

Title 知愧軒尺牘 *Chih Kúei Hsüan Chih Tu*

Classification *D—43*

Subject

References
                                          (Shanghai, Wang Ting-Hsüeh (Tzŭ-Chih)
                                          revised

Author 吳縣管斯駿秋初著 *Wu-Hsien, Kuang Ssŭ-Chün (Chiu-Chǔ)*
長洲，姚印詮暘奇注，上海，王廷學子芝校 *Cháng-Chou, Yao Yin-Chüan (Ir-Chai) and*

Edition 光緒戊子年上海尚五山房重校刊 *Dated Kuang-Hsü "Wu-Tzǔ" Shanghai, Chien-Yü-Shan-Fang
                                          1888*

Index 綿連紙 *"Mien-Kien" paper*

Bound in *1 tǎo, 16 chüan, 4 tsé*

Remarks 硃批 初珍本

The University of Toronto Chinese Library

....

Accession No. *1961*   Index No. *075·ah30*

Title　本朝文讀本　*Pên Chao Wên Tu Pên*

Classification　*D-73*　　總集，文

Subject

References

Author　清馬俊良讀　*Chíng, Ma Chün-Liang*

Edition　小倉山房原本　*Hsiao-Tsang-Shan-Fang original copy*
　　　　白紙　　　　　*white paper*
　　　　熙春堂藏　　　*Hsi-Chün-Tang Preserved edition*

Index

Bound in　*4 tsé*

Remarks

The University of Toronto Chinese Library

. . . .

Accession No. 1962   Index No. 140-P3ie

Title 蘇黃趙帖 Su Huang Ti Po

Classification C-223 叢書（子部 藝術類）

Subject

References

Author 宋蘇東坡，黃山谷 Sung, Su Tung-Po and Huang Shan-Ku

Edition 又賞齋藏板 Yu-Shang-Chai block preserved edition
乾隆五十年鶴，綿連紙
Dated Chien-Lung 15/1785 "Mien-Lien" paper

Index

Bound in 1 t'ao, 5 ts'ê (5 chüan)

Remarks

The University of Toronto Chinese Library

....

Accession No. 1963   Index No. 085-9386

Title 涇川叢書 *Ching chüan Tsung Shu*

Classification C - 338

Subject

References

Author 清, 趙星閣 撰刻 *Written & engraved by Ching, Chao Hsing Ko.*

Edition 道光壬辰年刊 *Dated:- Tao Kwang "jên-chên" period Preserved.*
古墨齋藏板 *Block-preserved in Ku-mo-chai.*

Index

Bound in 4 函 24 Tsè.

Remarks

The University of Toronto Chinese Library

....

Accession No. *1964*   Index No. *086-ihce*

Title 熙朝紀政 *Hsi Chao Chi Cheng*

Classification *B—32* 紀事苐末

Subject *Complete historical narratives of "Ching" dynasty*

References

Author 清, 王慶云著 (慶) (given in oral by) *Ching, Wang Ching-Yün*

Edition 石印印 光緒年印 連史紙
Lithographic edition, dated Kuang-Hsü period (1875-1908)
"Lien-Shih" paper

Index *A general table of content for 6 chüan*

Bound in *1 t'ao, 6 chüan, 6 ts'e*

Remarks

Accession No. *1965*   Index No. *086-ihce*

Title 熙朝紀政 *Hsi Chao Chi Chêng*

Classification *B-32* 紀事專集

Subject *Complete historical narrative of "Ching" dynasties*

References

Author 清, 慶 王京云(?) *given in Oral by Ching, Wang Ching-Yün*

Edition 石印, 光緒年印 選光緒
Lithographic edition, dated Kuang-Hsü period (1875-1908)
"Lien-Shih" paper

Index *a general table of contents for 6 chüan*

Bound in *1 t'ao, 6 chüan, 6 tsê*

Remarks

The University of Toronto Chinese Library

. . . .

Accession No. *1966*   Index No. *075-3ch*

Title 校字譜 *Hsiao Tzŭ Lu*

Classification *A — 151* 小學

Subject *A dictionary with examples for explanation*

References

Author 清, 文泙寺普等, *Written by* *Ching, Shih Ping and others*

Edition 中將年 巨老七卅刊, 毛巴珠
       Chin Hsiang Pên
       Pocket edition, dated Tao-Kuang 7/1827

Index   *"Mao-Pien" paper*
       A general table of all the radicals according to number of strokes.

Bound in *1 tʻao. 2 tʻsê*

Remarks

The University of Toronto Chinese Library

. . . .

Accession No. 1967   Index No. 149-ge

Title 說鈴 Shuo Ling

Classification C-308

Subject

References

Author 清 名家雜著 Ching, Ming Chia _Several_ Famous Writers

Edition 清嘉慶四年巳未重鐫
    Dated — Chia-Ching "Chi-Wei" 4/1799

Index

Bound in 2 t'ào 10 ts'è

Remarks

Accession No. *1968*   Index No. *149-2037*

Title 談藝珠叢 *Tan I Chu Tsung*

Classification ~~D 藝 珠 叢~~ 7 D 43

Subject

References

Author 清, 王灝采輯 *Compiled by Ching. Wang Chi-yüan*

Edition 長沙玉尺山房刊本 光緒乙酉年刊, 綿連紙 *Chang-Sha, Yü-Chih-Shan-Fang edition, dated Kuang-Hsü "I-Yu"/1885 "Mien-Lien" paper*

Index *a general table of contents for 44 chüan*

Bound in *1 t'ao, 44 chüan, 10 ts'e*

Remarks

The University of Toronto Chinese Library

. . . .

Accession No. 1969 A-B   Index No. 125-3 m h3

Title 老學庵筆記 二卷   滿清官場百怪錄 二卷
Lao Hsüeh An Pi Chi Êrh Chüan   Man Ching Kuan Chǎng Pai Kuai Lu
                                                    Êrh Chüan
Classification C - 387

Subject

References

Author ¹宋 陸游著   ².雲間顥公著
Sung, Lu Yu ; Yün Chien Tien Kung

Edition 掃葉山房石印   1.宣統三年 2.民國二年
Sao Yeh Shan-Fang
Dated One in Hsüan-Tung "Hsin-Hai" 3/1911
         One in Ming-Kuo 2/1913
Index

Bound in 1 tào   6 ts'ê

Remarks

207

The University of Toronto Chinese Library
. . . .

Accession No. 1970　　　　　Index No. 182/jhze

Title 馭橋日記 Fan Lun gih Chi

Classification D—43 引華—文

Subject an individual diary

References

Author 清 李厚滋著 Ching. Li Hou-Tzu

Edition 家藏石印刻 連史紙

Private family lithographic edition
"Lien- Shih" paper

Index None

Bound in 1 tao, 2 Chüan, 2 Ts'è

Remarks

The University of Toronto Chinese Library

....

Accession No. 1971   Index No. 030—bbзʉ
Title 古今小品 Ku Chin Hsiao Pin

Classification δ

Subject

References

Author 陳天定評選 Selected by Chén Tïen Ting Ping

Edition 几水書院藏版
Chi Shui school Preserved.

Index

Bound in 八卷附鄉薰題目四卷八冊

Remarks 竹紙 Bamboo Paper
夾板 Wooden folder

209

The University of Toronto Chinese Library

. . . .

Accession No. *1972*　　　　Index No. *085·湘湘湘*

Title 湘綺樓箋啟　*Hsiang I Lou Chien Chi*

Classification *D—43 別集一元*

Subject *individual collections of letters*

References

Author 王闓運著　*Wang Kai-Yün*

Edition 上海廣益書局發行

　　　Shanghai, Kuang-I Book Company

Index *a general table of contents for 8 chüan*

Bound in *1 t/ao, 8 chüan, 4 t'sê*

Remarks

The University of Toronto Chinese Library

．．．．．．．．．．．．．．．．．．．．．．．．

Accession No. 1973   Index No. 086-i 九 ce

Title 熙朝紀政 Hsi Chao Chi Chêng

Classification B—32 紀事专苦

Subject Complete historical narratives of "Ching" dynasties.

References

Author 清. 王先之(王庆) Given in oral by Ching, Wang Ching-Yün

Edition 上海古局館印, 老情年印, 松[重]印,
Shanghai Book Company type-setting edition
dated Kuang-Hsü period (1875-1908), "Fên-Lien"-paper

Index A general table of contents for 8 chüan

Bound in 1 t/ao, 8 chüan, 4 tsê

Remarks

The University of Toronto Chinese Library

. . . .

Accession No. 1974   Index No. 172-丁马 d

Title 離垢集 Li Kou Chi

Classification D-38 別集一等

Subject an individual collection - g poetry

References

Author 華齋著 Hua Chai (著)

Edition 依藏版. 羅嘉志重刊, 錦連紙
Private family edition, Lo Chia-Chieh (重刊) Reprinted edition.
"Mien-Lien" paper

Index none a general table g contents for 5 chüan

Bound in 1 t'ao, 5 chüan, 4 ts'e

Remarks

The University of Toronto Chinese Library

....

Accession No. 19 7 5 ^18   Index No. 031-カカda

Title 國朝先正事略 *Kuo Cháo SHsien Chêng Shih Lüeh*

Classification β-117

Subject

References

Author 清 李元度纂 *Compiled by* *Ching, Li Yüan-Tu*

Edition 山東官印書局校印本 *Shan Tung, Kuang Yin book company revised*
洋粉連紙 *Western "fên Lien" paper* *imported*

Index

Bound in 2 tao, 10 Ts'ê 60 chuan

Remarks

The University of Toronto Chinese Library

. . . .

20

Accession No. 1976   Index No. 077-lccz

Title 歷代名臣言行錄 Li Tai Ming Chen Yen Hsing Lu

Classification B-117

Subject

References

Author 清 朱恒編輯 Compiled by Chíng, Chu Hêng

Edition 上海商務印書館 Shanghai, Shang Wu book company
鉛印本 洋紙 Type-setting ed.
imported Western paper

Index

Bound in   9 ts'e   24 chuan

Remarks

The University of Toronto Chinese Library

. . . .

55

Accession No. 1977   Index No. 085-2ce

Title 清代軼聞 *Ching Tai I Wên*

Classification B-52 (子部)

Subject

References

Author 裴鋭麟著 *Chiu Yü-Lin*

Edition 上海中華書局鉛印本 *Shanghai, Chung Hua book company*
Type-setting ed.
洋紙　民國四年印 *Dated — Ming-Kuo 4 /1915*
imported Western paper

Index

Bound in   10 *chuan*   4 *ts'è*

Remarks

. . . .

Accession No. 1978   Index No. 120-008

Title 續同書 Hsü Túng Shu

Classification C-303

Subject

References

Author 清 福禹門輯 Compiled by Ching, Fu Yü-Mên

Edition 道光十九年刊
Dated — Tao-Kuang "Chi-Hai" 19/1839

Index

Bound in 1 táo   6 tsè

Remarks

. . . .

131

Accession No. 1979   Index No. 072-又gad

Title 普通百科新大辭典 *Pʻu Tʻung Pai Kʻo Hsin Ta Tz̆ü Tien*

Classification A-161

Subject

References

Author 清 黃摩西編輯 *edited & Compiled by* Chʻing, Huang Mo-Hsi

Edition 中國詞典公司鉛印 *China Chung Kuo, Tzü-Tien-Kung Ssü* *type-setting ed.*

宣統三年版 油光紙
辛亥

Index Dated — Hsüan-Tung "Hsin-Hai" 3/1911
"Yu Kuang" paper

Bound in 2 tao   15 tsʻê

Remarks

The University of Toronto Chinese Library

. . . .

Accession No. *1980*   Index No. *199-03ck*

Title 讀書紀數略 *Tu Shu Chi Shu Lüeh*

Classification *C-308*

Subject

References

Author 清 宮定山編 *edited by* *Ching, Kung Ting-Shan*

Edition 殿版 康熙四十六年 *J荒* *Palace ed.*
  Dated —— Kʾang-Hsi "Ting-Hai" 46/1707

Index

Bound in *2 tʾao   16 tsʾa*

Remarks

The University of Toronto Chinese Library

....

Accession No. 1981   Index No. 117-3383

Title 章氏叢書 Chang Shih Tsung Shu

Classification c-338

Subject

References

Author 章太炎著 Chang Tai-Yen

Edition 上海右文社印行
Shanghai, Yu-Wên-Shê published

Index

Bound in 4 tao 23 tsi

Remarks

Accession No. 1983   Index No. 167-3んっC

Title 金陵瑣志三種 *Chin Ling So Chih San Chung*

Classification B-217

Subject

References

Author 陳作霖 *Chén Tso-Lin*

Edition 光緒庚十正月
光緒乙酉仲夏新鐫
板藏金陵治麓山房
Pan Tsang Chin Ling Yeh Lu Shan Fang

Index *Dated Kuang-Hsü "I-Yu 11/1885*

Bound in 1 *Tao*, 2 *ts'è*

Remarks

220

The University of Toronto Chinese Library

· ·

Accession No. *1985*   Index No. *001-b01c*

Title 三續疑年錄 *San Hsü I Nien Lu*

Classification *B — 22* 傳奇

Subject *a record of hundards of the well-known* Chinese people
age —— Date of births + deaths.

References

Author 清, 陸心源 輯 edited by *Ching, Lu Hsin-Yüan*

Edition 家藏版, 光緒手刻, 白紙
~~Private family~~ Private *edition, dated Kuang-Hsü period (1875-1908)*
white paper

Index *no index*

Bound in *1 t'ao, 10 chüan, 2 ts'e*

Remarks

. . . .

Accession No. 1986   Index No. 085—9d66

Title 海忠介公集 Hai Chung Chieh Kung Chi

Classification D

Subject

References

Author 明海瑞撰 *Written by* Ming, Hai Shui

Edition 家藏版 Private *family* printed edition

Index

Bound in 六卷二冊 6 Chuan 2 Tsé

Remarks 綿連紙 Mien Lien Paper

222

The University of Toronto Chinese Library

....

Accession No. 1987   Index No. 094-ㄥㄇㄌㄐ

Title 猗覺寮雜記 I Chüeh Liao Tsa Chi

Classification C-13

Subject

References

                      Written by
Author 宋 朱翌撰 Sung, Chu I

Edition

Index

Bound in 1 t'ao 2 ts'ê

Remarks

The University of Toronto Chinese Library

. . . .

Accession No. 1988   Index No. 149-9323

Title 誡子庸言 Chieh Tzŭ Yüng Yen

Classification C—13 儒家

Subject Family education + discipline

References

Author 清, 莫祺川著 Ching, Mo Ching-Chuan

Edition 家藏版, 双面連紙, 木版
private family edition, "Shuang-Mien-Lien" paper, woodenblock

Index No index

Bound in 1 套, 2 冊

Remarks

224

The University of Toronto Chinese Library

. . . .

Accession No. *1989*   Index No. *009-李𢌿𢙐*

Title 傳經室文集 *Chuan Ching Shih Wên Chi*

Classification *刀 — 43 别集 — 文*

Subject *an individual collection of prose*

References

Author 清, 朱駿聲 *Written by* 撰, *Ching, Chu Chün-Shêng*

Edition 幺/尺 古悠齋 刊, 竹紙, 木板.

    Liu-Shih, Chiu-Shu-Chai edition, Bamboo paper, wood block

Index *a general table of contents for 10 chüan*

Bound in *1 tào, 10 chüan,* 附錄考 *1 chüan, 2 tsê*

Remarks   *Attached "Fu" 1 chüan*

225

The University of Toronto Chinese Library

． ．

Accession No. *1990*   Index No. *042-3 m 2 j*

Title N. 小學弦歌   *Hsiao Hsüeh Hsüan Ko*

Classification *D 6 8 38*

Subject

References

Author 清，平江李元度 *輯*   *compiled by* *Ch'ing, P'ing-Chiang, Li Yüan-Tu*

Edition 光緒八年秋月 文昌書局重刊 毛太紙
Dated Kuang-Hsü 8 autumn 1882   "Mao T'ai" paper
Wên-Chang Book Company revised edition

Index

Bound in / *t*ậo 5 *t*ậ̂*

Remarks

The University of Toronto Chinese Library

. . . .

Accession No. 1991   Index No. 120-09k

Title 纂理窟 *Hsü Li Ku*

Classification と─308 韓文

Subject 正風格破遺信員守科さねぶ样

References

Author 清, 李木林著 *Ching, Li Ta-Fi*
李問渔 *Wen yu*

Edition 上海土山湾印書館館船印大写字 澤白洋紙

Shanghai, *Tú-Shan-Wan-Yin-Shu-Kuan* printed, Big
characters, ~~they white western~~ imported paper

Index *a general table of contents*

Bound in *1 t'ao, 2 ts'è.*

Remarks

Accession No. 1993   Index No. 024—9 k m a

Title 南豐劉先生文集 Nan Feng Liu Hsien Sheng Wen

Classification D   Chi

Subject

References

Author 清劉孝經撰 Written by Ching, Liu Fou Ching

Edition 上海聚珍仿宋印書局印
Shanghai chü Chen Fang Sung Book Co. Printing.

Index

Bound in 四卷 附補遺 四冊

Remarks 毛边紙 Mao-Pien Paper

228

The University of Toronto Chinese Library

. . . .

Accession No. 1994   Index No. 085-dg il

Title 汪穰卿遺著 Wang Jan Ching yi chu

Classification δ

Subject

References

Author 清汪康年著 汪詒年編次 Ch'ing, Wang Kang Nien,

Edition 家藏版 Private family edited in order by Wang I. Nien. printed edition.

Index

Bound in 八卷四冊 8 Chuan 4 Tsê

Remarks 白毛边紙）
White Mao Pien paper.

The University of Toronto Chinese Library

. . . .

Accession No. 1995   Index No. 075-3dgd

Title 桂林梁先生遺書 Kuei Lin Liang Hsien Shêng I Shu

Classification D-23

Subject

References

Author 清 梁巨川著作 Ch'ing, Liang Chü-Ch'uan

Edition 民國十四年 京華書局印制
        Ching-Hua book company published
    Dated — Ming-Kuo 14/1925

Index

Bound in 1 t'ao 4 ts'ê

Remarks

The University of Toronto Chinese Library

. . . .

Accession No. *1996*   Index No. *001-a2*

Title 七克 *Chi Ko*

Classification *C—971*

Subject

References

Author 清 龐迪我 撰 *Written by* *Ching, Pang Ti-O*

Edition 京都始胎大堂藏版 油光紙, 木版
Ching-Tu, Shih-Tai-Ta-Tang *Preserved edition* *Yu-Kuang" paper, wood block*

Index

Bound in *1 tào, 7 Chüan, 4 tsè*

Remarks

Accession No. *1997*   Index No. *161-793元*

Title 農圃頌譯 *Nung Pŭ So Tan*

Classification 乙一53

Subject

References

Author 清 楊景仁等撰, 龍博霖輯 *Lung Pu-Lin* (輯)(Compiled)
Written by *Ching, Yang Ching-gên and others* (撰) (Compiled)
Edition 桂林 唐九地堂刊 光緒六年刊 綿連紙
Kuei-Lin, Táng-Chiu-gu-Táng, dated Kuang-Hsü 6/1880 "Mien-Lien" paper

Index

Bound in / 套 2 *t'sê*

Remarks

232

The University of Toronto Chinese Library

. . . .

Accession No. *1999*   Index No. *048-bkgi*

Title 左傳事緯 *Tso Chuan Shih Wei*

Classification *A— 101*

Subject

References

Author 清, 馬驌撰 *Written by Ching, Ma Hsiu*

Edition 敬慎堂刊 光緒年刻 竹紙
Ming-Tê-Tâng block-engraving edition, Dated Kuang. Hsii period / 1875-1908.
Bamboo paper

Index

Bound in *2 t'ao, 12 ts'e*

Remarks

234

The University of Toronto Chinese Library

· ·

110

Accession No. 2002   Index No. 085-ec3p

Title 治安文獻 Chih An Wên Hsien

Classification B-72(?)

Subject

References

Author 清 韓訥 韓壽名 輯 Compiled by Ch'ing, Han No, Han Shou Ming

Edition 家藏版 寫刻本 Private- family ed. printed Manuscript
毛邊紙 "Mao Pien" paper

Index

Bound in 2 tao   10 chuan   11 ts'ê

Remarks

235

The University of Toronto Chinese Library

. . . .

Accession No. 2003   Index No. 146-3²79

Title 西湖佳話 Hsi Hu Chia Hua

Classification B—212 地理— 古蹟

Subject Historical geography and archaeology of the "Western Lake" Hangchow

References

Author

Edition 金陵王街梓版 精繪沒色全圖
Block-preserved
Chin-Ling Wang-Ya edition, fine plain colored pictures

Index a general table of contents for 16 Chüan

Bound in 1 t'ao, 16 Chüan, 8 t'ee

Remarks

The University of Toronto Chinese Library

．．．．．．．．．．．．．．．．．．．．．．．

Accession No. 2004   Index No. 037-aLai

Title 天崇百篇 Tien Chung Pai Pien

Classification D—43 鑑葉一文

Subject *Selections from the prose writings of ancient scholars with commentary.*

References

Author 清，吳懋政選輯， *Selected & Compiled by* Chiag. Wu Mao-Chêng

Edition 學庫山房刊，光緒年刊，竹紙
Hsüeh-Ku-Shan-Fang edition, dated Kuang-Hsü period (1875-1908)
Bamboo paper

Index *a general table of contents for 4 Chüan*

Bound in *1 t♮o, 4 Chüan, 4 t'ê*

Remarks

The University of Toronto Chinese Library

. . . .

?

Accession No. 2006   Index No. 134- *l hmg*

Title 舊聞隨筆 *Chiu Wên Sui Pi*

Classification β-117

Subject

References

Author 清 姚永樸著 *Ching, Yao Yung-Pú*

Edition

Index

Bound in 1 *tao*, 1 *ts'ə*

Remarks

239

Accession No. 2007   Index No. 037-a&dg

Title 太祖皇帝大破明師於薩爾滸山之戰書事文
Tai Tsu Huang Ti Ta Po Ming Shih Yü Sa Êrh Hu Shan Chih Chan Shu Shih Wên

Classification B-52

Subject

References

Author

Edition 殿板 Palace ed.

Index

Bound in 1 t'áo 1 ts'ê

Remarks 滿文漢文合刊

The University of Toronto Chinese Library

....

Accession No. 2008   Index No. 085-2n2p

Title 河嶽英靈 Ho Yü Ying Ling

Classification D — 38 别集, 一卷

Subject An individual collection of poetry; a historical writing.

References

Author 清, 衞河世書 Ching, Wei Chi-Shih

Edition 全一堂叢板. 戊午辛亥年鑑, 印世板
Chu-I-Táng edition, dated Hsien-Fêng "Hsin-Hai" /1851
'Mien-Lien' paper

Index None

Bound in 1 t'ao, 6 chüan, 4 ts'ê

Remarks

241

The University of Toronto Chinese Library

· ·

Accession No. 2009   Index No. 075-idib

Title 楊忠愍公全集 Yang Chung Min Kung Chüan Chi

Classification ﾉ-23

Subject

References

Author 明 楊繼盛著 Ming, Yang Chi-Shêng

Edition 道光元年重刊　思補堂藏板
　　　　　辛巳
　　　　　　　Ssǔ-Pu-Táng printed. block preserved ed.
Dated —— Tao-Kuang "Hsin-Ssǔ" 1/1821 Reprinted edition

Index

Bound in 1 t'ao 4 ts'ê

Remarks

The University of Toronto Chinese Library

· ·

88

Accession No. 2010   Index No. 032-lezd

Title 增刪卜易 Tsêng Shan Pu I

Classification A-11

Subject

References

Author 野鶴老人著 Yeh-Ho-Lao-gen

Edition 文成堂刊 Wên-Chêng-Tâng published block-engraving.
竹紙 bamboo paper

Index

Bound in 1 t'ao   6 chuan   4 Ts'ǒ

Remarks

243

The University of Toronto Chinese Library

. . . .

Accession No. 2011   Index No. 030-bb 傳

Title 古今類傳 Ku Chin Lei Chuan

Classification c-348

Subject

References

Author 清 董農山 董霞山 輯 *Compiled by* Ching, Tung Nung-Shan, Tung Hsia-Shan

Edition 康熙壬申年刊 未學齋藏板 *block preserved edition.*
Wei-Hsüeh-Chai ~~private printed~~
Dated — Kang-Hsi "Jên-Shen" 31/1692

Index

Bound in 1 t'áo 4 ts'ê

Remarks

244

The University of Toronto Chinese Library

....

Accession No. 2012   Index No. 106-dhje

Title 皇朝諡法考 *Huang Chao Shih Fa Kao*

Classification β287

Subject

References

Author 趙之謙署檢 歙鮑康輯 王鵬運輯
Chao Chih-Chien Shu-Chien (compiled by) Hsi Pao-Kang; Wang Péng-Yün

Edition 清 同治三年甲子十二月刊
光緒十六年重刊
Dated — first edition — Ching, Tung-Chih "Chia-Tzŭ"
                                    3/1864 December.

Index   *Second edition — Kuang-Hsü "Kêng-Ying" 16/1890*

Bound in 1 tao, 5 chuan, 1 ts'ê

Remarks

The University of Toronto Chinese Library

. . . .

Accession No. 2013   Index No. 102-29 Ji

Title 異號類編 I Hao Lei Pien

Classification 乙一348一穀t'

Subject a kind of encyclopedias

References

Author 清, 史夢蘭 輯, Compiled by Ching, Shih Mêng-Lan

Edition 止園藏板, 同治乙丑年刊, 竹紙
Chih-Yüan edition, dated Tung-Chih "I-Chou"/1865, Block preserved
Bamboo paper

Index a general table of contents for 20 chüan

Bound in 1 t'ao, 20 chüan 4 ts'ê

Remarks

The University of Toronto Chinese Library
. . . .

Accession No. 2014　　　　Index No. 181-2233

Title 漁潭詩話　Wan Tan Shih Hua

Classification D-38 別集－詩文

Subject an individual collection of prose poetry; with commentary

References

Author 清 陳珣輯　Compiled by　Ching, Chên Hu

Edition 崑山趙氏小帆樓校刻本 毛邊紙　Collated black
Kun-Shan, Chao-Shih, Hsiao-Fan-Lou　second printed edition
"Mao-Pien" paper

Index

Bound in 1 t'ao, 4 chüan, 2 ts'è

Remarks

The University of Toronto Chinese Library

. . . .

Accession No. 2015   Index No. 061-dzbl

Title 念一史彈詞注 Nien I ~shih~ Tan Tzǔ Chu

Classification B — 12 已失

Subject collections of commentaries on the twenty-one
(21) officially approved and authorized standard
dynastic histories of China ; in poetic writings

References

Author 明, 楊愼著 Compiled by ~Ming, Yang Shên~

Edition 私葬版. 乾隆年刊. 竹紙
~Private~ ~family~ ~Hand~ edition, ~dated~ Chien-Lung period (1736-1795)
Bamboo paper

Index a chronological table of contents for 2 chüan

Bound in 1 t'ao, 2 ts'e, 2 chüan

Remarks

248

The University of Toronto Chinese Library
....

Accession No. 2016   Index No. 060-hhjd.

Title 御製圓明園圖詠 Yü Chih Yüan Ming Yüan Tu Yung

Classification C-223 D-38

Subject

References Toronto Nos. 776, 1508

Author 清世宗著 Ching, Shih Tsung — Emperor Yung-Chêng

Edition 光緒十三年天津石印書屋摹勒上石
丁亥   Tientsin, Shih-Yin-Shu-Wu Mo-Lê-Shang-Shih
Dated — Kuang-Hsü "Ting-Hai" 13/1887

Index

Bound in 1 t'ao   2 ts'ê

Remarks

The University of Toronto Chinese Library

. . . .

Accession No. 2017   Index No. 155-39 hi

Title 赤城論諫錄 *Chih Chêng Lun Chien Lu*

Classification B一22 道公秦濤一秦濤

Subject

References

Author 明 謝鐸等編 *Ming, Hsieh To and others*

Edition 四庫全書本,台州叢書續編內,毛邊紙
Ssŭ-Kú-Chüan Shu Pên, Tái-Chou Tsung Shu Hsü Pien,
"*Mao - Pien*" paper

Index *a general table of contents for 10 chüan*

Bound in *1 hó, 10 Chüan, 2 tsĕ*

Remarks

250

The University of Toronto Chinese Library

. . . .

Accession No. 2018   Index No. 118-3230

Title 竹居小牘 Chu Chü Hsiao Tu

Classification D-43 別集-文   Pieh Chi — Wên (Individual
                                        collection - prose)
Subject an individual collection of letters in
        prose.

References

Author 濤樓主人佛存 Tao-Lou-Chu-Jên

Edition 竹居刊本, 綿連紙
        Chu-Chü Kan Pe edition, "Mien-Lien" paper

Index A general table of contents for 12 Chüan

Bound in 1 t'ao, 12 Chüan, 2 tse

Remarks

251

The University of Toronto Chinese Library

....

Accession No. 2019   Index No. 162-2m

Title 大學 Shu Hsüeh

Classification C-13

Subject Philosophy Explanation of the Classics & philosophy

References

Author 清, 江中棅, Written by Ching, Wang Chung

Edition 吳葆根, 錦連纸 Private family library edition, "Mien-Lien" paper

Index

Bound in / t'ao, 2 t'sè

Remarks

The University of Toronto Chinese Library

. . . .

Accession No. Jr 2020   Index No. 027-h3bi

Title 原人內篇 Yüan Jên Nei Pien

Classification C—308

Subject Philosophy

References

Author 皖江, 陳劍潭先生撰 Written by Huan-Chiang, Chen Chien-Tan

Edition 晦室叢書之一 — Huei Tang Tsung Chu Chih I
民國十二年   Dated Republic 12/1923

Index Sperate index for each "Chüan"

Bound in 1 t'ao, 2 ts'ê

Remarks

253

Accession No. 2022   Index No. 106-d kje

Title 皇朝謐洁表   Huang Chao Shih Fa Piao

Classification B-287

Subject

References

Author 清 楊樹編   edited by
                      Ching, Yang Shu

Edition 克緒二十六年三月刊
Dated — Kuang-Hsü "Jên-Ying" 28/1912 March

Index

Bound in 1 tao, 2 ts'ê

Remarks

The University of Toronto Chinese Library

. . . .

26,48

Accession No. 2023   Index No. 030-bb 8

Title 古今僞書考考釋 Ku Chin Wei Shu Kao Kao Shih

Classification B-337

Subject

References

Author 清 姚晉源原著   金受辛弦釋
       Ching, Yao Shou-Yüan. Chin Shou-Tzǔ (commentary)

Edition 鉛印本 中華書局 印刷局 Chung Hua Shu Chü Press Co.
        民國十三年初版 厚毛邊紙 Type-setting edition
                              Thick "Mao-Pien" paper
Index   Dated — Ming-Kuo 13 / 1924

Bound in 1 t'ao   2 ts'ê

Remarks

The University of Toronto Chinese Library

. . . .

Accession No. 2024 A-B   Index No. 018-2273
                                           018-22K3
Title 刪定荀子   Shan Ting Hsün Tzŭ
      刪定管子   Shan Ting Kuan Tzŭ
Classification C-13

Subject

References

Author 清.方苞 刪定 Ching, Fang Pao

Edition 平湖屈氏藏本, 綿連紙, 夾板
        Ping-Hu, Chü-Shih, Preserved
        private edition
        "Mien-Lien" paper, Woodenblock folder
Index no idex

Bound in (A) 1 tsê   1 tao
         (B) 2 tsê
Remarks

The University of Toronto Chinese Library
. . . .

Accession No. 2025   Index No. 178-jzkz

Title 藍山堂文集 Yün Shan Táng Wên Chi

Classification D—33—別集—詩文

Subject an individual collection of prose and poetry

References

Author 清. 管世駱 撰 Written by Ching, Kuan Shih-Ming

Edition 清雪山房藏版 光緒20年重鎸 毛邊紙
Tu-Hsüeh-Shan-Fang block preserved edition, dated Kuang-Hsü 20/1894
"Mao-Pien" paper

Index a list of work for 8 chuan

Bound in 1 t'ao, 8 chuan, 2 ts'ê

Remarks

The University of Toronto Chinese Library
. . . .

Accession No. 2026 A-B   Index No. 039-a ji d

Title 孔子編年 四卷   孟子編年 四卷
        K'ung Tzŭ Pien Nien   Mêng Tzŭ Pien Nien
                    Ssŭ Chüan   Ssŭ Chüan
Classification c-13

Subject

References

Author 清 狄子奇撰 *Written by* Ch'ing, Ti Tzŭ-Chi

Edition 光緒丁亥年浙江書局刻
        Chê-Chiang Sha Chü Book Co.
    Dated — Kuang-Hsü "Ting-Hai" 13/1887

Index

Bound in 1 t'ao   2 ts'ê

Remarks

258

The University of Toronto Chinese Library

. . . .

12

Accession No. 2028   Index No. 030-czci

Title 同音字辨 Tʻung Yin Tzŭ Pan ? Pien

Classification A-156

Subject

References

Author 清 劉維坊彙輯 Compiled by Chʻing, Liu Wei-fang

Edition 重訂本 Rebound ed. 京師善定成堂藏板 Ching-Shih, Shan-Chʻêng-Tʻang first printed 同治十二年刊 竹紙 block preserved ed.

Index Dated — Tʻung-Chih "Kuei-Yu" 12/1873 Bamboo paper

Bound in 1 tʻao   4 chuan   4 tsʻe

Remarks

259

The University of Toronto Chinese Library

· ·

Accession No. 2029   Index No. 075-ill

Title 楚辭燈 *Chu Tzu Têng*
    一燈

Classification D — 14

Subject

References

Author 清．林雲銘 論註 *given in oral by Ching, Lin Yün-Ming*

Edition 挹奎堂藏板 毛太紙 *block preserved*
Ching-Kuo-Tang edition, "Mao-Tai" paper

Index

Bound in 1 tho, 4 Chüan, 2 tsê

Remarks

260

The University of Toronto Chinese Library
· ·

Accession No. 2030   Index No. 072-zbih

Title 日下尊聞錄 Jih Hsia Tsun Wên Lu

Classification C —— 238 親板鄉 301 雜葉

Subject 解辭名勝古蹟

References

Author

Edition 安和軒樣板, 咸豐手刻, 竹紙, 木板
blak preserved
An-Ho-Hsüan, edition, dated Hsien-Fêng (1851-1861),
period
Bamboo paper, woodenblock

Index no index

Bound in 1 t'ao, 5 chüan, 2 ts'ê

Remarks

Accession No. 2031 A-B   Index No. 030-b8, 149-0bb3

Title 史筌 二卷 讀史論略 二卷   Shih Chüan   San Chüan
                                          Tu Shih Lun Lüeh   Erh Chüan

Classification 3-267

Subject

References Toronto 2047 A-B

Author 清 楊銘桂編 edited by n Ching, Yang Ming-Chu

Edition 道光二十六年刊 寄雲書屋藏板 block-preserved ed.
兩午   Chi-Yün Wu-Shu-Wu private-printed

Dated — Tao-Kuang "Ping-Wu" 26/1846

Index

Bound in 1 t'ao 4 ts'e

Remarks

The University of Toronto Chinese Library

. . . .

Accession No. 2032   Index No. 120-Chhi

Title 紅樓夢偶說 Hung Lou Mêng A. Ou Shuo

Classification C-368

Subject

References

Author 晶三蘆月草舍居士著   簣覆山房主人編次
       Ching San Lu Yüeh Tsou Chü Shih. Kuei Fu Shan Fang Chu Jen

Edition 清光緒二年刊   板藏簣覆山房
          丙子   Pan Tsang Kui-Fu-Shan-Fang private library

        Dated — Kuang-Hsü "Ping-Tzu" 2/1876

Index

Bound in 1 tʻáo   2 tsʻê

Remarks

263

The University of Toronto Chinese Library

· ·

2

Accession No. 2033   Index No. 009.mmme

Title 儀禮釋官 I Li Shih Kuan

Classification A-51

Subject

References

Author 清 胡匡衷著 Ching, Hu Kuang-Chung

Edition 嘉慶丙子年刊 竹紙 Bamboo paper
Dated — Chia-Ching "Ping-Tzu" 21/1816

Index

Bound in 9 Chuan, 2 ts'ê

Remarks

The University of Toronto Chinese Library

. . . .

Accession No. 38
2034   Index No. 072-dcza

Title 明李文正公年譜 Ming Li Wên Chêng Kung Nien Pu

Classification B-107

Subject

References

Author 清 法式善纂輯 Compiled by Ching, Fa Shih-Shan

Edition 家藏版 Private-printed family edition
嘉慶年重刊 竹紙 Bamboo paper
Dated — Chia-Ching period 1796—1820 Reprinted ed.

Index

Bound in 1 t'ao 7 chuan 2 ts'ê

Remarks

. . . .

26

Accession No. 2035   Index No. 062-ℓ27c

Title 戰國策去毒 Chan Kuo Tsê Chü Tu

Classification B-2552

Subject

References

Author 清 陸隴其輯 Compiled by Ching, Lu Lung-chi

Edition 六安求我齋重刊本 Liu-An, Chiu-O-Chia re-published printed ed.

同治庚午年刊 連綿紙

Index Dated — Tung-Chih "Kêng-Wu" 9/1870 "Mien Lien" paper

Bound in 1 t'ao   2 chuan   2 ts'ê

Remarks

The University of Toronto Chinese Library
....

Accession No. 2036   Index No. 156-g²98

Title 趙註孫子 Chao Chu Sun Tzŭ

Classification C-33

Subject

References

Author 明 趙廬舟注 Annotated by Ming, Chao & Hsü-Chou

Edition 原本蓟遼舊刻   清代重刻   赤西齋藏板 & block preserved ed.
        Su-Liao Original copy   I-Hsi-Chai private printed
        Second ed. — Ching period 1653 — 1911
                    Dynastic Rep. Re-engraved ed.

Index

Bound in 1 t'ao 4 tsi̇́

Remarks

The University of Toronto Chinese Library

. . . .

Accession No. 2037　　　　　Index No. 031·ㄥㄥㄥ m

Title 國朝漢學師承記，附宋學淵源記

Kuo Chao Han Hsüeh Shih Chêng Chi　*Fu Sung Hsüeh Yüan Yüan Chi*

Classification ㄥ — 13

Subject

References

　　　　　　　　　　　　　Compiled by
Author 清，江 藩纂，*Ching, Chiang Fan*

Edition 萬卷書室藏板 光緒十三年新鐫
　　　　　　　　block preserved
Wan-Chüan-Shu Shih, edition, dated *Kuang-Hsü 13/1887*

Index

Bound in 1 *t'ao*, 4 *ts'ê*

Remarks

The University of Toronto Chinese Library

....

Accession No. 2038   Index No. 018-X39k ^m

Title 刘氏家塾四書解 Liu Shih Chia Shu Ssŭ Shu Chieh

Classification A——131 四書

Subject *commentary writing on the Four Books*

References

Author 清, 袁文雄校刊, *Collated edition by* Ching, Yüan Wen-Huan

Edition 家塾齋板, 光緒丙子年刊, 竹紙 *Private school Home edition, dated Kuang-Hsü "Ping-Tzŭ" /1876 Bamboo paper*

Index *none*

Bound in / 套, 8 冊

Remarks

The University of Toronto Chinese Library

. . . .

Accession No. 2139   Index No. 099-3⁴3c

Title 甘棠小志 Kan Tang Hsiao Chih

Classification β—194 引志

Subject Local gazeteers with maps.

References

Author 清, 董醇著 Ching, Tung Chun

Edition 吳斋版, 咸丰辛刻, 也乞紙

Private family edition, dated Hsien-Fêng period (1851-1861),
   "Lien-Shih" paper

Index a general table of contents for 4 chuan & a
   separate table of contents for each chuan.

Bound in 1 t'ǎo, 4 chuan, 4 ts'è

Remarks

270

The University of Toronto Chinese Library

. . . .

Accession No. 2041   Index No. 072-ed79

Title 春秋取義(以) Chün Chiu Chü I Tsê

Classification A.—101

Subject

References

Author 清, 清坤弼宏樑 Written by Ching, Fa Kung-Hung

Edition 粵省西湖奇六書奇刻, 精密刻本
乾隆甲寅手刻 綿連紙
Canton, Hsi-☆Hu-Chai, Liu Shu Chai printed, fine printed
"Mien Lien" paper, dated Chien-Lung "Chaia-Yin"/1794 manuscript edition
Index

Bound in / Tho, 12 Chüan, 4 Tsê

Remarks

271

The University of Toronto Chinese Library

. . . .

Accession No. 2043   Index No. 096-9k

Title 理窟 Li Kü

Classification C—971

Subject

References

Author 清 李林著 Ching, Li Ti

Edition 上海土山灣印書館法版 大字本 洋紙
Shanghai, Tú-Shan-Wan book company. Big characters edition large
imported
foreign paper
Western

Index

Bound in 1 tào, 9 chüan, 2 tsè

Remarks

The University of Toronto Chinese Library

. . . .

Accession No. 2044   Index No. 069-inʒh

Title 新疆建置志. *Hsin Chiang Chien Chih Chih*

Classification B-192

Subject

References

Author 清 宋伯魯撰 光緒三十四年 *Written by Ching, Sung Po-Lu*

Edition 民國二年胡文濬發行 *Wu Hu-Wên-Chʽan*
海棠仙館板
Hai-Tʽang Hsien-Kuang official edition
Dated — Ming-Kuo 2/1913

Index

Bound in 1 tʽao   4 chuan   4 tsʽê

Remarks

The University of Toronto Chinese Library

. . . .

Accession No. 2045   Index No. 089-jdoa

Title 爾雅讀本 Ênh Ya Tu Pên

Classification A-156

Subject

References

Author 清周樽輯 Compiled by ching, chou Tsun

Edition 家藏版 Private-printed family edition
竹紙 Bamboo paper

Index

Bound in 4 Chuan, 2 ts'ê

Remarks

Accession No. 2047 A-B   Index No. 030-b8; 149-0627

Title 史筌三卷 讀史論略二卷   Shih Chüan   San Chüan   Tu Shih Lun Lüeh   Êrh Chüan

Classification B-367

Subject

References

Author 清 楊銘柱編   edited by   Ching, Yang Ming-Chu

Edition 道光二十六年刊 兩字 寄雲書屋藏板 block preserved ed.   Chi.Yün-Shu-Wa private printed
Dated — Tao-Kuang "Ping-Wu" 26/1846

Index

Bound in   1 táo   2 tsʼǒ

Remarks

275

The University of Toronto Chinese Library

. . . .

Accession No. 2048   Index No. 030-deah

Title 呂祖太極先生數 Lü Tsu Tái Chi Hsien Shêng Shu

Classification C－985

Subject

References

Author 金桂抄錄 Chin Kuei copied

Edition 道光年寫, 紅格寫, 弄板
    Dated Tao-Kuang period (1821-1850)
    "Hung-ko" paper, woodenblock
Index printed in red columns.

Bound in 1 thọ, 2 t'sê

Remarks

276

The University of Toronto Chinese Library

• •

Accession No. 2050   Index No. 149-kzmz

Title 課子隨筆鈔 Ko Tzŭ Sui Pi Chao

Classification C—308 雜文

Subject ~~collection~~ collection from the writings of some 70 authors,
of homiletical writings

References

Author 傅村 張又渠 輯 Compiled by I-Fêng, Chang Yu-Chü

Edition 家藏版 Private family House edition

Index a general table of contents for 6 chüan—

Bound in 1 t'ao, 6 ts'ê, 6 chüan, continue one more chüan

Remarks

277

Accession No. 2053   Index No. 085-大引引

Title 漢書蒙拾   Han Shu Mêng Shih

Classification B-367

Subject

References

Author 清 杭世駿鈔撮 Ch'ing, Hang Shih ch'ün Ch'ao Tsô

Edition

Index

Bound in 1 t'áo   3 ts'è

Remarks

Accession No. 2054   Index No. 033-3d0c

Title 士林藝訓 Shih Lin I Hsün

Classification c — 308 群考一 中群文

Subject A collection of ~commentary on~ philosophy and other ancient writings in four ~parts~ sections :—
1. Study & learning 2, ethics 3, individual personality 4, adjustment in the world.

References

Author 清, 開槐士 ~Given in oral by~ Ching, Kuan Huai

Edition 廣東院署藏板 ~block preserved~ 印代
Kuang-Tung-Yüan-Shu edition, Bamboo paper

Index A general table of contents for 8 chüan

Bound in 1 t/ao. 8 chüan, 2 t'ê

Remarks

The University of Toronto Chinese Library

· ·

Accession No. 2055   Index No. 036.K938

Title 夢窗甲乙丙丁稿 Mêng Chuang Chia I Ping Ting Kao

Classification D—113 詞曲 一 詞集

Subject an individual collection of lyrics.

References

Author 宋, 吳文英 撰. Written by Sung, Wu Wên-Ying

Edition 王佑(遐)仿宋刊校, 光緒年刊 綿連紙
engraved blocks
Wang Yu-Hsia immitated Sung edition
dated Kuang-Hsü period (1875-1908)
"Mien-Lien" paper

Index a general table of contents for 4 chüan 甲乙丙丁. Chia, I, Pin, Ting

Bound in 1 t'ao. 4 chüan, 6 ts'ê

Remarks

280

The University of Toronto Chinese Library

. . . .

Accession No. 2057   Index No. 203-d7

Title 黔書   Chien Shu

Classification B — 1922共 地理, 東志

Subject ~~History of~~ a gazetteer for the province 貴K
                                                    -chow

References

                    edited by
Author 清. 田雯編ₙ Ching, Tien Wên

Edition 黔滕使者太湖李重鑅, 嘉木戊長手刻
        貴州綿紙, 木版
        Chien-Fan Shih Chê, Tai-Hu, Li Chung edition, dated chia-ching
        "Wu-Chên"/1808, "Kui-Chou Mien" paper, woodenblock.

Index a general table of contents for 2 Chüan

Bound in / tao, 2 Chüan, / 帙

Remarks

The University of Toronto Chinese Library

....

Accession No. 2058   Index No. 128-Pdj8

Title 聽訟彙案 Ting Sung Hui An

Classification 乙一43 信案

Subject 審判各種案件之記載

References

Author 日车東陽津阪孝建輯
Written by Japan, Tung-Yang-Ching-Pan-Hsio-Cho
Edition 日车稽古精舍版, 高麗紙, 一朵版
     Japan, Chi-Ku-Ching-Shê edition, Korean paper, wood block

Index none

Bound in / t/ao, 3 chüan, 3 t'ê

Remarks

282

The University of Toronto Chinese Library

. . . .

Accession No. 2059   Index No. 085-hʒde

Title 添品妙法蓮華經 Tien Pin Miao Fa Lien Hua Ching

Classification C-513

Subject

References

Author 隋 天竺闍那崛多共達摩笈多添品譯
Sui Tien Chu Tu Na Chüeh To Kung Ta Mo chi To Tien Pin translated

Edition No date

Index

Bound in 1 táo 2 tsʻė́

Remarks

The University of Toronto Chinese Library

....

Accession No. w060 P118   Index No. 122·nicz

Title 羅鄂州小集 Lo O Chou Hsiao Chi

Classification D—33 刮集一淳文

Subject an individual collection of prose and poetry.

References

Author 明, 羅端良撰, Written by Ming, Lo Tuan-Liang

Edition 影錄李氏竹明洗井专重刊 光猪某七年刊, 竹竹紙
I-Hsien Li-Shih imaitated Fang Ming Hung-Wu's copy
Dated Kuang-Hsü "Kui-Ssü" /1893, Bamboo Paper

Index a general table of contents for 6 chüan—

Bound in / tao. 6 chüan, 2 tse

Remarks

284

The University of Toronto Chinese Library

. . . .

Accession No. 2061   Index No. 001—6gie

Title 三教搜神大全 *San Chiao Sou Shen Ta Chüan*

Classification C—731

Subject

References

Author 清葉德輝仿元版重刊

Edition Ch'ing. Yeh Tê-Hui imitation of Yüan blocks reprinted

宣统元年刻 block-engraving in the first year of "Hsüan-Tung"

Index 連史纸 Lien shih paper

Bound in 7 Chüan 2 tao

Remarks

285

Accession No. 井 2062   Index No. 113-cim

Title 社會學 Shê Hui Hsüeh

Classification D—153 群部—哲枕濟寺

Subject ~~Sociology~~ General principles of Sociology

References

Author 呂復著 Lü Fu

Edition 北京 中國印刷局印, 民國十六年印, 連史紙
Peking, Chung-Kuo-Yin-Shua-Chü printed, dated Republic 16/1927
"Lien-Shih" paper

Index a table of contents for 4 Chüan

Bound in 1 t'ao, 4 ts'ê, 4 Chüan

Remarks

The University of Toronto Chinese Library
....

Accession No. 2064   Index No. 118-3129

Title 竹葉亭雜記 Chu Yeh Ting Tsa Chi

Classification C－318 雜家 — 雜文 (Miscellaneous writing)
                    Tsa Chia — Tsa Wên

Subject Miscellaneous writings

References

Author 清. 姚元之著 Ching, Yao Yüan-Chih

Edition 原 刊版. 光緒年刊. 竹紙紙
Private family edition, dated Kuang-Hsü period (1875-1908)
Bamboo paper

Index a table of contents telling the No. of writings in
each chüan

Bound in 1 t'ao, 8 chüan, ♯ 2 ts'e

Remarks

287

The University of Toronto Chinese Library

....

Accession No. 2065   Index No. 030·93·9

Title 唐人萬首絕句選 Táng Jên Wan Shou Chüeh Chü Hsüan

Classification D — 68 詩集一 清

Subject A general collection of poetry in "Tong" dynasty

References

Author 宋·洪邁原本, 清·王士禎批

Sung, Hung Mai's original copy; Ching, Wang Shih-Chên (批) compiled by

Edition 初印本, 雍正癸丑48年刊, 毛邊紙

first printed edition ∧ dated Yüng-Chêng "Jên Tzŭ"/1732

"Mao-Pien" paper

Index A list of the no. of writers of each chüan.

Bound in 1 t'ho, 9 chüan, 2 tsè

Remarks

288

The University of Toronto Chinese Library

. . . .

Accession No. *2066*   Index No. *142-gbcd*

Title 蛻私軒集 *Tó Ssǔ Hsüan Chi*

Classification *D-33*

Subject

References

Author 清 姚永樸著 *Ching, Yao Yung-Pu*

Edition 辛酉年秋浦周氏刊行
Pú-Chou-Shih
Ching Dynastie 1644 - 1911

Index

Bound in *1 táo   1 tsǎ*

Remarks

Accession No. 2067   Index No. 072-dgm

6

Title 易通釋 通例 I Túng Shih Túng Li

Classification A-11

Subject

References

Author 清 陳啓彤著 ching, Chên chi-Túng

Edition 家藏版 Private-printed family edition
洋毛邊紙 imported Western "Mao Pien" paper

Index

Bound in 3 Chuan, 3 tsê (通釋 2 Chuan, 通例 1 Chuan)

Remarks

The University of Toronto Chinese Library

....

Accession No. 2069

Index No. 077-1c88

Title 歷代帝王年表 附帝王廟諡年諱譜

Li Tai Ti Wang Nien Piao

Classification B-187

Fu Ti Wang Miao Shih Nien Hui Pu

Subject

References

Author 清　齊照南編, edited by Ching, Chi Chao-Nan

Edition 小瑯環仙館刊 Hsiao-Lang-Huan-Hsien-Kuang

光緒年刻　綿連紙 "Mien Lien" paper

Index Dated — Kuang-Hsü period 1875—1908

Bound in 1 t'ao 4 ts'ê

Remarks

The University of Toronto Chinese Library

....

Accession No. 2070   Index No. 073-k399

Title 曾子家語 Tsêng Tzŭ Chia Yü

Classification C-13

Subject

References

                        edited by
Author 清, 王定安 編 Ching, Wang Ting-An

Edition 光緒十六年刊本
        Dated: Kuang-Hsü 16/1890 block-printed edition

Index

Bound in 1 t'ào, 2 ts'é

Remarks

The University of Toronto Chinese Library

....

Accession No. 2071 A-B   Index No. 128-93 kg

Title 聖門樂誌, 聖門禮誌, Shêng Mên Yüeh Chih
                              Shêng Mên Li Chih

Classification B-287

Subject

References

Author

Edition 光緒丁亥重刊
        板藏闕里硯寬亭
        Pan Tsang Chüeh-Li-Yen-Kuan-Ting private library
Index   Dated — Kuang-Hsü "Ting-Hai" 13/1887 Rep Re-engraving
                                              Re-Engraved.

Bound in 1 tao, 2 ts'ǔ

Remarks

The University of Toronto Chinese Library

· ·

Accession No. 2072   10   Index No. 037-38mc

Title 大戴禮記斠補 *Ta Tsai Li chi Chüeh Pu* / *Chiao*

Classification A-56

Subject

References

Author 清孫詒讓撰 *Written by Ching, Sun I-jang*

Edition 廣明印刷兩石印本 *Kuang Ming Yin Shuai So press co. lithographic ed.*
連史紙 *"Lien Shih" paper*

Index 3 *chuan*

Bound in 1 *tao*, 3 *tsé*

Remarks

294

The University of Toronto Chinese Library

....

Accession No. 2073   Index No. 122-nicy

Title 羅鄂州小集　附鄂州遺文一卷
　　　　Lo Ao Chou Hsiao Chi
Classification D-38   Fu Ying Chou I Wên I Chüan

Subject

References

Author 宋　羅願著 Sung, Lo Yüan

Edition 光緒癸巳年黟縣李氏仿明洪武本重刊
　　　　　　　　　　　　　　revised
　　　　I-Hsien, Li-Shih ∧ Ming, Hung Wu's copy

　　　Dated — Kuang-Hsü "Kuei-Ssu" 19/1893

Index

Bound in 1 táo 2 ts'ê

Remarks

The University of Toronto Chinese Library

....

Accession No. 2024   Index No. 053-2279d
                                               Hsien
Title 康對山先生武功祿志. Káng Tui Shan She shêng Wu
                        Kung Hsien Chih

Classification B—194 地理 ┼ 祿志

Subject Local
       ∧Together of the count of "Wu-Kung"

References

                      Commenteds annotated by
Author 清,孫景烈評注. Ching, Sun Ching. Lieh

Edition 孫氏刻本 乾隆二十六年刊. 綿連紙
        Blockprint
Sun-Shih ∧edition, dated Chien-Lung 26/1761. "Mien-Lien" paper

Index a general table of content for 3 chüan

Bound in 1 t'ào, 2 t'sè, 3 chüan

Remarks

The University of Toronto Chinese Library

. . . .

67

Accession No. 2075   Index No. 070-38

Title 方言 Fang Yen

Classification A-156

Subject

References

Author 漢 揚雄記 Annotated by 晉 郭璞註

take notes by Han, Yang Hsiung; Chin, Kuo Pu

Edition 思賢講舍版 Ssŭ-Hsien Chiang Shê

光緒年刻 白紙 White paper

Dated — Kuang-Hsü period 1875-1908

Index

Bound in 十三卷 續二卷 2 ts'è

Remarks 13 Chuan, Continue 2 Chuan

297

The University of Toronto Chinese Library

. . . . : . . . .

Accession No. 2076   Index No. 085-mzc7

Title 澳門記略 *Ao Mêng Chi Lüeh*

Classification B-194 51/亏

Subject *Local gazeteers of "Macao"*

References

Author 清印光任等 Compiled by *Ching, Yin Kuang-jēn and others*

Edition 家藏版, 嘉慶五年刊, 綿連紙
Private family edition, Chia-Ching 5/1800, "Mien-Lien" paper

Index *a general table of contents for 2 chüan*

Bound in *2 t'ao, 2 chüan, 2 t'ae*

Remarks

298

The University of Toronto Chinese Library

. . . .

Accession No. 2077   Index No. 085-hdjl

Title 清芬樓遺藁 Chïng Fën Lou Yi Kao

Classification A

Subject

References

Author 清任啟運撰 Written by Chïng, Jao Ch'i Yün

Edition 家藏版 Private-printed family edition

Index

Bound in 四卷二冊 4 Chüan 2 Tsë

Remarks 光緒戊子年刻 Block engraving in Kuang Hsü "Wu Tzu" period
毛边紙 Mao-pien paper

The University of Toronto Chinese Library
· ·

Accession No. 2098,   Index No. 077-ami

Title 正學編 Chêng Hsüeh Pien

Classification C-308 郭景一郭大

Subject Miscellaneous writings & discussions.

References

Author 清, 潘世恩 輯 Compiled by Chîng, Pán Shih-Ên

Edition 家藏版, 向治六年刊, 綿連紙
Private Family Edition, dated Tüng-Shih 6/1867
"Mien-Lien" paper

Index None

Bound in / T'ao, 2 Tsè, 8 Chüan

Remarks

The University of Toronto Chinese Library

. . . .

Accession No. 2079   Index No. 010-d938

Title 先聖生卒年月日攷 Hsien Shêng Shêng Tsu Nien Yüeh Jih Kǎo

Classification B—117 詩/㡳 ㎞

Subject A general collected biographies 攷

References

Author 清, 3山廣校雅書, Gwen in Oral by Ching, Kung Kuang-Mu

Edition 廣雅書局刊, 光緒十五年刊, 毛邊紙
Kuang-Ya Book Company, dated Kuang-Hsü 15/1889
"Mao-Pien" paper

Index None

Bound in 1 t'ao, 1 tsê, 2 chüan   Prt 三先聖卒年表
Remarks   attached with "San Kuang Nien Piao"

The University of Toronto Chinese Library

. . . .

Accession No. 2080   Index No. 009-2mcg

Title 佛學地理志 Fo Hsüeh Ti Li Chih

Classification c-513

Subject

References

Author 張相文著 Chang Hsiang-Wên

Edition 民國十四年成 中國地學會出版 中華書局印
         China, Ti-Hsüeh-Hui, China, Chang-Hua Shu-Chü Book Co. publish
         Dated — Ning-Kuo 14/1925

Index

Bound in   1 táo   1 tsʾü

Remarks

302

The University of Toronto Chinese Library

· ·

Accession No. 2081 9

Index No. 120-9908

Title 經書字音辨要 Ching Shu Tzŭ Yin Pien Yao

Classification A-166

Subject

References

Author 清 楊名飏 編輯 edited & Compiled by Ch'ing, Yang Ming-Yang

Edition 令德堂重刻本 Ling-Tê-Táng Second ed. Re-block-print edition
道光丁未年刊 綿連紙
Index Dated — Too-Kuang "Ting-Wei" 27/1847 "Mien Lien" paper

Bound in 1 tao, 9 Chuan, 1 ts'ê (?)

Remarks

303

Accession No. 2082 ⁴

Index No. 120-9808

Title 經書字音辨要 Ching Shu Tzŭ Yin Pien Yao

Classification A-166

Subject

References

Author 清 楊名颺 撰 Written by Ching, Yang Ming-Yang

Edition 含德堂刻本 Ling-Tê-Tʻang block-print edition.
綿連紙 "Mien Lien" paper

Index

Bound in 1 tʻao. 9 chuan. 2 tsʻê.

Remarks

The University of Toronto Chinese Library

. . . .

Accession No. 2083   Index No. 075-d h d z

Title 東萊先生古文關鍵 Tung Lai Hsien Shêng Ku Wên Kuan Chien

Classification B-367

Subject

References

Author 呂祖謙評 Lü Tsu-Chien Commentaries.

Edition 清光緒戊戌年　江蘇書局刊版
Chiang·Su·Shu-Chü Book Co. engraved blocks.

　Dated — Ching, Kuang-Hsü 戊 Wu-Hsü 24/1898

Index

Bound in 1 t'ao 2 ts'ê

Remarks

305

The University of Toronto Chinese Library

. . . .

Accession No. 2084   Index No. 120-Cjc

Title 約園志、 Yüeh Yüan Chih

Classification D-53

Subject

References

Author 清 徐樹銘 輯 Compiled by Ching, Hsü Shu-Ming

Edition 光緒二十三年刊
Dated Kuang-Hsü "Ting-Yu" 23/1897 block engraving ed.

Index

Bound in 1 t'ao 3 ts'ê

Remarks

The University of Toronto Chinese Library

. . . .

Accession No. 2086   Index No. 009-ji

Title 人範 Jên Fan

Classification C-328

Subject

References

Author 清 蔣元輯 Compiled by Ching, Chiang Yüan

Edition 光緒辛丑年 廣雅書局重刊) reprinted edition
Kuang-Ya-Shu-Chü Book Co. re-published
Dated — Kuang-Hsü "Hsin-Ch'ou" 27/1901

Index

Bound in 1 t'ao 1 ts'ê

Remarks

307

The University of Toronto Chinese Library

．．．．．．．．．．．．．．．．．．．．．．．．

Accession No. 2088   Index No. 212-3743

Title 龍舒淨土文 Lung Shu Ching Tu Wên

Classification C-513

Subject

References

Author 龍舒居士王日休譔 Written by Lung Shu Chü Shih Wang Jih Hsiu Chuan

Edition 清康熙年刊
Dated — block engraving in Ching, Kang-Hsi period 1662—1722

Index

Bound in 1 t'ao   2 ts'ê

Remarks

308

The University of Toronto Chinese Library

. . . .

Accession No. 2089   Index No. 030-bp⅔c

Title 史鑑節要便讀 Shih Chien Chieh Yao Pien Tu

Classification B—12 正史

Subject official dynastic histories; in poetry style and with commentary

References

Author 清 鮑 古邨 編輯。 *edited & compiled by* Ch'ing, Pao Ku-Tsun

Edition 崇文書局, 同治年刊, 竹紙 *block-engraving in* Chúng-Wên Book Company, *dated* Tung-Chih period (1862-1874) Bamboo paper

Index none

Bound in 1 t'ao, 6 chüan, 2 t'ê

Remarks

The University of Toronto Chinese Library

. . . .

Accession No. 2090   Index No. 030-blcm

Title 古籟今學 Ku Tzŭ Ling Hsüch
                          chin

Classification C-328

Subject

References

Author 盧靖纂 Lu Ching
              Compiled by

Edition 民國十四年   慎始基齋叢書   聚珍板印 Movable-type ed.
              Shên-Shih-Chi-Chia Tsung Shu, Chü Chên Pan
         Dated — Ming-Kuo 14/1925

Index

Bound in 1 tào 2 tsè

Remarks

The University of Toronto Chinese Library
....

Accession No. 2091   Index No. 009-dc7h

Title 伊江筆錄 二編 I Chiang Pi Lu Enh Pien

Classification

Subject

References

Author 清 吳熊光著 Ching, Wu Hsiung-Kuang

Edition 廣雅書局印 Kuang-Ya Shu-Chü Book Co, published

Index

Bound in 1 t'ao 1 ts'e

Remarks

311

The University of Toronto Chinese Library

. . . .

Accession No. 2092   Index No. 118-扌kdʒ

Title 節盦先生遺詩 Chieh An Hsien Shêng I Shih

Classification D-38

Subject

References

Author 清 梁鼎芬著 Ch'ing, Liang Ting-fên

Edition 光緒十九年刊 block engraving in
Dated ── Kuang-Hsü "Kuei-Ssŭ" 19/1893

Index

Bound in 1 t'ao 2 ts'ê

Remarks

312

The University of Toronto Chinese Library

. . . .

30

Accession No. 2093   Index No. 030-bn4c

Title 史鑑節要便讀 Shih Chien Chieh Yao Pien Tu

Classification B-22

Subject

References

Author 清 鮑東里編輯 edited & Compiled by Ching, Pao Tung-Li

Edition 家藏版 重刊本 Private-printed family second edition
Reprinted edition
綿連紙 夾板 Wooden block
"Mien Lien" paper

Index

Bound in 1 t'ao   6 chuan   2 ts'ǒ

Remarks

The University of Toronto Chinese Library
. . . .

17

Accession No. 2094   Index No. 062-2238c

Title 戰國策去毒 Chan Kuo Tsê Chü Tu

Classification B-52

Subject

References

Author 清　陸隴其評選 Commented & selected by Ch'ing, Lu Lung-Chi

Edition 六安求我齋重刊本 Liu-An, Chiu O-Chia reprinted edition. re-published.

同治庚午年刊　綿連紙

Index "Mien Lien" Paper Dated — Tung-Chih "Kêng-Wu" 9/1870

Bound in 2 chuan 1 ts'ê

Remarks

314

The University of Toronto Chinese Library

．．．．．．．．．．．．．．．．．．．．．．

Accession No. 2096   Index No. 147-Rdzh

Title 觀世音菩薩大悲陀羅尼經咒
Kuan Shih Yin Pu Sa Ta Pei To Lo Ni Ching Chou

Classification C-513

Subject

References

Author

Edition 清 咸豐元年 按識本及 明萬曆二十九年刻本 刻成
Dated—Block-printed ed.——Ming, Wan-Li "Hsin-Chou" 29/1601
——Ching, Hsien-Feng "Hsin-Hai" 1/1851

Index

Bound in 1 t'ao   1 ts'e

Remarks

315

Accession No. 2096 ᵗᵇ   Index No. 037-azaj

Title 太子太傅先莊毅公東巖府君年譜
Tái Tzǔ Tái Fu Hsien Chuang I Kung Tung Yen Fu Chün Nien Pú

Classification B-107

Subject

References

Author

Edition 家藏版 Private-printed Family edition
同治癸年刊於廣州 夾連紙
Published in Canton "Chia Lien" paper

Index Dated — Tung-Chih "Kǎng-Wu" 9/1870

Bound in 1 t'ao 2 ts'ŭ

Remarks

Accession No. 34 2097   Index No. 075-ij dz

Title 楊園先生年譜 Yang Yüan Hsien Shêng Nien Pu

Classification B-107

Subject

References

Author 清 姚夏輯 Compiled by Ching, Yao Hsia

Edition 家藏版 Private-printed family edition
白紙 White paper

Index

Bound in 1 tao 4 chuan (附錄一卷) 1 ts'a

Remarks

317

The University of Toronto Chinese Library

. . . .

Accession No. 2098   Index No. 115-273m

Title 秦書八體原委 Chin Shu Pa Ti Yüan Wei

Classification A—161—字書

Subject a commentary on the "Chinese Writing"
Complet collection and

References

Compiled by
Author 清華學疎軒 Ching, Hua Hsüeh-Su

Edition 天津博物院影印寫与

Tientsin. Po-Wu-Yüan photolithographic edition

Index No index

Bound in 1 本, 2 本

Remarks

The University of Toronto Chinese Library

. . . .

Accession No. 2099   Index No. 064-dkzn

Title 折獄龜鑑 Chê Yü Kuei Chien

Classification 乙一43 庆岳

Subject 審判各种案件之记載.

References

Author 宋, 鄭克東書 Sung, chêng Kô-Yüan

Edition 山陽李氏問均香室所集刻)
匡光十五年刻, 佛连纸 木版
Shan-Yang, Li-shih, 'Wên-Miao-Hsiang-Shih printed edition
dated Tao-Kuang 15/1835, "Mientien" paper, wood-block

Index a general table of contents for 8 chüan

Bound in 1 t'ao, 8 chüan, 2 t'sê

Remarks

319

The University of Toronto Chinese Library

· ·

Accession No. 2100   Index No. 053-9c33

Title 庭訓格言 Ting Hsün Ko Yen

Classification C-13

Subject

References

Author 清聖祖皇帝制 made by Ch'ing Shêng-Tsu Emperor

Edition 殿板 Palace ed.

Index

Bound in 1 t'ao   1 ts'ê

Remarks

The University of Toronto Chinese Library

. . . .

44

Accession No. 2101   Index No. 057-bkbc

Title 弘毅公行慶錄 附戰功行略
Hung I Kung Yen Ching Lu
Classification B-107   Fu Chan Kung Hsing Lüeh

Subject

References

Author 清 額宜都巴圖魯曾孫愛必達纂
Compiled by Ching, O I Tu Pa Tu Lu Tseng Sun Ai Pi Ta
Edition 家藏版 Private printed Private family edition.
綿連紙 "Mien Lien" paper

Index

Bound in 1 tao, 4 ts'ê, 12 chuan.

Remarks

321

28

Accession No. 2102   Index No. 037-3 h c e

Title 大清同治四年歲次乙丑時憲書
Ta Ching Tung Chih Ssŭ Nien Sui Tzŭ I Ch'ou Shih Hsien Shu

Classification B-157

Subject

References

Author

Edition 硃墨寫本 Multi-color Manuscripts in red + black
開化榜紙 "Kai Hua Pang" paper Paper made in "Kai Hua Pang"

Index

Bound in 1 t'ao   1 ts'ê

Remarks

322

The University of Toronto Chinese Library
· ·

Accession No. 2103   Index No. 030-biih

Title 古意新情 Ku I Hsin Ching

Classification C.308 雜家-雜定

Subject

References

Author 日本西師意 Janpan, Hsi Shih-I

Edition 李茂棠印刻 Li-Mao-Táng printed
         雙綿連紙 "Shuang-Mien-Lien" paper

Index

Bound in 1 táo 1 ts'e

Remarks

Accession No. 2105   Index No. 141-glgd

Title 虞德園先生集 Yü Tê Yüan Hsien Shêng Chi

Classification 子-43 D-38

Subject

References

Author 清 虞淳熙著 Ching, Yü Chün-Hsi

Edition

Index

Bound in 1 t'ao 4 ts'ê

Remarks

The University of Toronto Chinese Library

. . . .

Accession No. 2106   Index No. 180-3332

Title 音韻逢原 Yin Yün Fêng Yüan

Classification A-166

Subject

References

Author 清 裕恩 撰定 *Written by* Ch'ing, Yü Ên

Edition 聚珍堂列 Chü-Chên-T'ang

道光年刻 毛邊紙

Index Dated — Tao-Kuang period 1821—1850 "Mao Pien" paper

Bound in 1 t'ao, 12 chüan, 4 ts'ê

Remarks

The University of Toronto Chinese Library

. . . .

Accession No. 2107   Index No. 050-hcdg

Title 常州先哲遺書 (詩傳旁通附三續十文詮)
Cháng Chou Hsien Chê I Shu (Shih Chuan Páng Túng Fu San Hsü Chien Wên
Classification C-338   chu)

Subject

References

Author 清 盛宣懷 彙刊 ∩Ching, Shêng Hsüan-Huai
                        Collected by

Edition 光緒二十五年 影印文瀾閣傳抄本
Photo-lithographic ing from "Lan-Ko Chuan Manuscript ed.
Dated — Kuang-Hsü "Chi-Hai" 25/1899

Index

Bound in 1 t'ao   2 ts'ê

Remarks

The University of Toronto Chinese Library

....

Accession No. 2108 A+B   Index No. 009-3 方 j
009-3 方 c

Title 人譜, 人譜類記 Jên Pu, Jên Pu Lei Chi

Classification 乙 — 308 雜書 — 專記文

Subject miscellaneous writings

References

Written by

Author 明, 刘宗周 撰, ∧ Ming, Liu Tsung-Chou

Edition 湖北崇文書局開雕, 光緒 三年, 連史紙
Hu-Pei, Chung-Wên Book Company
Dated Kuang-Hsü 3/1877.   "Lien-Shih" Paper

Index none 人譜 1 chüan, 人譜類記 6 chüan
Jên Pu   Jên Pu Lei Chi

Bound in 1 t'ao, 3 t'ĉê,

Remarks

327

The University of Toronto Chinese Library

· ·

Accession No. 2109   Index No. 131-k330

Title 臨文便覽 / Lin Wên Pien Lan

Classification A — 151 小學一詁音

Subject   Phonetic and graphic dictionaries

References

Author 清, 龍翰臣等撰。 Written by Ching. Lung Han-chên and others

Edition 同治甲戌年刊, 綿連紙
        Dated Tung-Chih "Chia-Hsü"/1874
        "Mien-Lien" paper

Index   none

Bound in 1 tǎu, 2 tsê

Remarks

328

The University of Toronto Chinese Library

· · · · · · · · · · · · · · · · · · ·

Accession No. 2110   Index No. 075-iggc

Title 楞嚴自知錄錄 Lêng Yen Tzŭ Chih Lu

Classification ∂513 釋家 Shih Chia

Subject

References

Author 清王麟印錄 Printed & copied & by ∧ Ching, Wang Lin

Edition 家藏本 ~~Home edition~~ Private family editions
康熙戊辰年刻 dated Kang. Hsi "Wu-Chên" /1688
錦連紙, 灭板 "Mien-Lien" paper, wood block

Index

Bound in 1 tʻao 2 tse

Remarks

329

The University of Toronto Chinese Library

. . . .

Accession No. 2114   Index No. 077-a m i

Title 正學編 Chêng Hsüeh Pien

Classification C-13

Subject

References

Author 清 潘世恩輯 *Compiled by* Ching, P'an Shih-Ên

Edition 道光三年刊 鳳池園藏板
block preserved in Fêng-Chih-Yüan *private printed*
Dated —— Tao-Kuang "Kuei-Wei" 3/1823

Index

Bound in 1 t'ao 1 ts'ê

Remarks

The University of Toronto Chinese Library

. . . .

Accession No. 2116   Index No. 072-彡八乙彡

Title 睨笑堂竹莊畫傳 *Wan Hsiao Tang Chu Chuang Hua Chuan*

Classification C-223

Subject

References *Toronto No. 2115*

Author 清 周上宮畫 其弟々撰刻
Ching, Chou Shang-Kuan

Edition 乾隆年刊
Dated — Chien-Lung period 1736-1795

Index

Bound in *1 tāo. 2 tséʔ*

Remarks

The University of Toronto Chinese Library

· ·

Accession No. 2119   Index No. 040- lm k l

Title 寫禮廎遺著 四種 Hsieh Li Chin I Chu Ssŭ Chung

Classification 叢部

Subject an individual collection of prose & poetry

References

Author 清. 王懿榮著 Ching, Wang Sung-Wei

Edition 鳧澤王氏刊, 共四種. 竹紙
Fu-Hsi, Wang-Shih edition. Four types
Bamboo paper

Index a general table of contents for 2 tie

Bound in 1 tao, 2 tie

Remarks

332

The University of Toronto Chinese Library

· ·

Accession No. 2120   Index No. 060-khjd

Title 御製大雲輪請雨經 Yü Chih Ta Yün Lün Ching Yü Ching

Classification C-513

Subject

References

Author 金簡 奉旨校刊 Collated edition by Chin Chien

Edition 清 乾隆四十七年 殿板 Palace edition
Palace ed.
Dated — Ching, Chien-lung "Jên-ying" 47/1782

Index

Bound in 1 táo 2 tsü

Remarks

333

The University of Toronto Chinese Library

....

Accession No. 2121   Index No. 030-2988

Title 味餘書室隨筆 Wei Yü Shu Shih Sui Pi

Classification C-308

Subject

References

Author 清 朱珪等奉旨錄 ‸Copied by Ching, Chu Kui and others

Edition 殿版 嘉慶庚申刊 Palace ed.
       Dated — Chia-Ching "Kêng-Shen" 5/1800

Index

Bound in   1 t'ao   2 ts'ê

Remarks

The University of Toronto Chinese Library

· ·

Accession No. 2123   Index No. 085-933e

Title 浙西水利備考 Chê Hsi Shuei Li Pei Kao

Classification B — 207 山川 Shan Chüan (Mountains and rivers)

Subject writings the rivers in western "浙江 Chê-chiang"
(with maps)

References

                              Compiled by
Author 清, 王鳳生纂 Ching, Wang Fêng-Shêng

Edition 仿影閣刊, 道光四年刊, 綿連紙
        Fan-Ying-Ko edition, Dated Tao-Kuang 4/1824
        "Mien-Lien" paper

Index none

Bound in / 套, / 匣

Remarks

The University of Toronto Chinese Library

....

Accession No. 2125   Index No. 118-3299

Title 竹葉亭雜記 Chu Yeh Ting Tsa Chi

Classification C-308 雜家,一雜文 (Miscellaneous
                        Tsa Chia   Tsa Wên   Writing)

Subject miscellaneous writings

References

Author 清, 姚元之著 Ching, Yao Yüan-Chih

Edition 係藏版, 光緒年刻, 竹紙
Private family edition, Dated Kuang-Hsü period (1875-1908)
Bamboo paper

Index a general table of contents for 8 chüan telling the No.
of writings in each chüan.

Bound in 1 t'ao, 8 chüan, 2 ts'ê

Remarks

336

The University of Toronto Chinese Library

. . . .

Accession No. 2126   Index No. 69-ibci

Title 新史合編直講 Hsing Shih Ho Pien Chih Chiang

Classification B—42 計末

Subject unclassified histories of Christianity

References

Author

Edition 土山灣印書館 鉛印本 洋紙 1913年印
Tú-Shan-Wan Company. Type-setting ∧ Western Paper, ∧ 1913 printed
'edition imported   + dated

Index a general table of contents for 20 chüan

Bound in 1 t'ao, 20 chüan, 10 ts'e

Remarks

The University of Toronto Chinese Library
....

Accession No. 2127   Index No. 120-9332

Title 經言枝指 Ching Yen Shih I

Classification A——11-句經

Subject A collection of commentaries of on "I-Ching" book of changes

References

Author 清, 徐文靖 著 Ching, Hsü Wen Ching

Edition 老宁堂藏版 乾隆丙子年刊, 竹紙印
Chih-Ning-Tông black preserved edition, dated Chien-lung "Ping-Tzu" 1756
Bamboo paper

Index A general table of contents for 14 Chüan

Bound in 1 t&v, 14 Chüan, 4 t&e

Remarks

The University of Toronto Chinese Library

. . . .

Accession No. 2128   Index No. 167-hch

Title 綴中綴 Tso Chung Tso

Classification D – 147 戲曲

Subject a collection of librettos

References

Author

Edition 懷情堂藏佛 道光己丑年鑑，陕建屁
Huai Ching Tang ~~edition~~ *Block Preserved.*, dated Tao-Kuang "己 chi Chóu"/1829
"Mien-Lien" paper

Index a general table of contents for 2 tse

Bound in 1 t'ao, 2 t'se

Remarks

339

The University of Toronto Chinese Library

. . . .

39

Accession No. 2129   Index No. 212-7981

Title 龔氏家譜 *Kung Shih Chia Pu*

Classification B-107

Subject

References

Author 清 龔守正撰 *Written by* *Ching, Kung Shou-Chêng*

Edition 家藏版 *Private-printed family edition*
綿連紙 *"Mien Lien" paper*

Index

Bound in 1 *tao* 2 *ts'ê*

Remarks

340

The University of Toronto Chinese Library

. . . .

Accession No. 2130   Index No. 140-509a

Title 蘿藦亭札記 Lo Mo Ting Tsa Chi

Classification 乙—308 雜著—雜文

Subject miscellaneous writings of the ancient writings

References

Author 清 徐鼒橋 抄 梂 Copied by Ching, Hsü Kou-Chiao

Edition 家藏版. 同治年刻. 棻紙

Private facsimile edition, dated Tung-Chih period (1862-1874)
"Fên" paper

Index none

Bound in / t'ao, 8 chüan, 4 ts'ê

Remarks

341

Accession No. 2133   Index No. 118-1334

Title 篆文金剛經 Chuan Wên Chin Kang Ching

Classification

Subject

References

Author 田潜寫 Copied by Tien Chien

Edition 辛酉年刊 Dated — "Hsien-yu"

Index

Bound in 1 t'ao 1 ts'e

Remarks

The University of Toronto Chinese Library

. . . .

Accession No. 2134   Index No. 075.78d3

Title 桐城吳氏點勘十三 Tùng Chêng Wu Shih Tien Kàn Shih Tzŭ

Classification C — 13, and 43, 931 + others 楊子, 法子, (莊子)等

Subject a collection of Philosophy, Jurisprudence, Taoism and others.

References

Author 清, 吳汝綸點勘 Ching, Wu Ju-Lun

Edition 引星社鉛印 宣統二年刊, 池史紙
Yen-Hsing-Shê type-setting edition, dated Hsüan-Tùng 2/1910
"Yü-Kuang" paper

Index a general table of content for 12 thae, a separate table of contents for each "Chia"

Bound in 2 thao, 12 thae

Remarks

343

The University of Toronto Chinese Library

. . . .

Accession No. 2135   Index No. 072-dzah

Title   明文才調集 Ming Wên Ts'ai Tiao Chi

Classification ~~R-43~~ ~~D-43~~ 別集 D-43 總集一文

Subject

References

Author 清 許振禕集。 Collected by Ch'ing, Hsü Chên-~~Wei~~ I.

Edition 大梁東河行署刊本 Ta-Liang Tung-Ho Hsing-Shu block print edition
光緒辛卯年刊 dated Kuang-Hsü "Hsin-Mao" 1891
竹紙。 Bamboo paper

Index none

Bound in 1 t'ao 4 ts'ê

Remarks

The University of Toronto Chinese Library

. . . .

Accession No. 2136   Index No. 159-bkj

Title 軍樂稿 Chün Yüeh Kao

Classification C-228

Subject

References

Author 清 李映庚 訂 Ch'ing, Li Ying-Kêng

Edition 宣統元年刊 石印版 Lithographic ed.
         Dated — Hsüen-Tung "Chi-yu" 1/1909

Index

Bound in 1 t'ao   4 ts'ê

Remarks

The University of Toronto Chinese Library

. . . .

Accession No. 2137   Index No. 146-зhdg

Title 西國近事彙編 Hsi Kuo Chin Shih Hui Pien

Classification 新部 B-227 地理-外記

Subject ~~the~~ events + relations
historical news ~~of~~ all foreign countries with
China during the last 100 years.

References

Author 美國林樂知口譯, 沈禁錫齡筆述
         Lin Lo-chih (American) translated orally (口譯), Chiny Tsai Hsi-Ling
Edition 活印本, 毛邊紙.   wrote
                                                    (筆述)
         Type-setting edition, "Mao-Pien" paper

Index none

Bound in 2 t'ao, 8 t'sê

Remarks

346

The University of Toronto Chinese Library

· ·

Accession No. 2138   Index No. 154 - d c c 3

Title 責志約言 Tsê Chih Yüeh Yen

Classification C - 328 雜家 — 雜纂

Subject

References

Author 清 王滌心著 Chíng, Wang Ti - Hsin

Edition 慎修堂藏版 Shên - Hsiu - Táng edition, blocks preserved.
咸豐五年刻 dated Hsien - Fêng 5/1855
連史紙, 夾板 "Lien - Shih" paper, wooden blocks

Index "Lien - Shih" Paper
none

Bound in 1 t'ao, 4 chüan, 4 tsê

Remarks

347

The University of Toronto Chinese Library

....

Accession No. 2139   Index No. 118·2ar3

Title 節本泰西新史攬要 *Chieh Pên Tai Hsi Hsin Shih Lan Yao*

Classification B-~~二一~~7 147

Subject

References

Author 英國李提摩太譯 *Timothy Li translated*

Edition 周慶雲節錄本 *Chou Ching-Yün*
　　　光緒辛丑夏 夢坡室刊成
　　　　　　　Mêng-Po-Shih

Index *Dated — Kuang-Hsü "Hsin-Chou" 27/1901 summer*

Bound in 1 tao, 2 ts'ê

Remarks

The University of Toronto Chinese Library

. . . .

Accession No. 2140   Index No. 010-b大dl

Title 之廣東書氏錄 Yüan Kuang Tung I Min Lu

Classification B—117 13花—錄鶴

Subject a collected biographies

References

Author 清湯溪陸嘉梓 Compiled by Ching, Hsi Yü-Yin

Edition 吳興版. 陸建瓜

Private family Hand edition, "Mien-Lien" paper

Index a general table of contents for a Chüan

Bound in 1 tào, 2 chüan, 2 t'cê

Remarks

2 30

Accession No. 2141 2141   Index No. 076-9888

Title 敕封大王將軍紀略 附畫像
Shu Fêng Ta Wang Chiang Chün Chi Lüeh
Classification B-107   Fu Hua Hsiang

Subject

References

Author 清 朱壽鏞 撰 Written by Ching, Chu Shou-Yung

Edition 石印本 Lithographic ed.
綿連紙 "Mien Lien" paper

Index

Bound in 1 tao, 2 ts'ê

Remarks

The University of Toronto Chinese Library

....

Accession No. 2142   Index No. 203-38c9

Title 黑龍江通志綱要 Hei Lung Chiang Tung Chih Kang Yao

Classification B142

Subject

References

Author 民國 金梁著 Chin Liang

Edition 民國年刊 Ming-Kuo

Index

Bound in 1 tao 2 tse

Remarks

The University of Toronto Chinese Library

....

Accession No. 2143 **Index No.** 049-3d h 3

Title 己亥談時 Chi Hai Tán Shih

Classification 乙——308 雜類—雜文

Subject Miscellaneous writing of the internal and external affairs of the Nation.

References

Author 清, 宋伯魯撰 Written by Ching, Sung Po-Lu.

Edition 海棠仙館原本, 鉛印大字, 洋紙 (characters) Hai-Tang-Hsien-Kuan original copy. Type-setting edition, big imported ~~Western~~ paper

Index none

Bound in 1 t'ao, 2 ch'üan, 2 ts'ê

Remarks

The University of Toronto Chinese Library
....

Accession No. 2144   Index No. 060-g3hi

Title 徐氏三种 Hsü Shih San Chung

Classification 丛部 C308

Subject

References

Author

Edition 京都，之成堂藏版，之清辛卯年重刻，竹纸
Ching-Shih, Wên Chêng-Tang edition
dated "Kuang-Hsü Hsin/Mao"/1891. Bamboo Paper

Index

Bound in 1 táo, 4 thê

Remarks

The University of Toronto Chinese Library

. . . .

Accession No. 2145   Index No. 005-aagg

Title 几几消夏錄 Chiu Chiu Hsiao Hsia Lu

Classification と-308 郒居-郒文

Subject a collection of writings of philosophy
literature, poetry, prose and others

References

                              Written by
Author 清, 俞樾 撰, Ching, Yü yüeh

Edition 学解册, 竹纸本

Private family Home edition, Bamboo paper

Index a general table of contents for 14 chüan

Bound in 1 t/30. 14 chüan, 2 ts'ê

Remarks

. . . .

Accession No. 2146   Index No. 096-zzgb

Title 王文敏公遺集 Wang Wen Min Kung I Chi

Classification 右

Subject

References

Author 清王懿榮著 Ching, Wang I Jung engraving

Edition 求恕齋刊 Chiu Shu Chai Block-Printing Edition

Index

Bound in 八卷二冊 8 Chüan 2 Tsê

Remarks 宣統年刻
竹紙 Bamboo paper
此書共有四部 4 volumes

Accession No. 2147   Index No. 007-cg

Title 五經 Wu Ching

Classification A-137

Subject

References

Author

Edition 金谷園藏板 Chin-Ku-Yüan private printed blocks-preserved edition.
清道光壬寅年鎸
Dated — Tao-Kwang "Jên-Ying" 22/1842

Index

Bound in 2 tao, 16 ts'ê

Remarks

The University of Toronto Chinese Library

. . . .

18

Accession No. 2148   Index No. 031-ʒʒʒʒ

Title 國朝御史題名錄 Kuo Chao Yü Shih Ti Ming Lu

Classification B-117

Subject

References

Author 清 黃玉圃 編輯。 *edited. compiled by* Ching, Huang Yü-Pu

Edition 京畿道藏版 Ching-Chi-Tao ~~private printed~~ *block preserved edition*
竹紙 Bamboo paper

Index

Bound in 1 t'ao   5 chuan   5 ts'ê

Remarks

The University of Toronto Chinese Library
. . . .

Accession No. 2149   Index No. 156-2909

Title 越南土也輿圖說 Yüeh Nan Ti Yü Tü Shuo

Classification B-227

Subject

References

Author 永新盛慶紱篹輯, Compiled by Yung-Hsin, Shêng Ch'ing-Fu

Edition 光緒九年秋
求忠堂藏板 blocks preserved
Chiu-Chung-Tang private printed ed.
Dated — Kuang-Hsü "Kuei-Wei" 9/1883

Index

Bound in 1 tao, 2 ts'ê (上,下)

Remarks

The University of Toronto Chinese Library

· ·

6

Accession No. 2150   Index No. 089-jdcz

Title 爾雅直音 Êrh Ya chih Yin

Classification A-161

Subject

References

Author 清 孫侃 輯 Compiled by Chíng, Sun Kán

Edition 崇德書院藏版 Chúng Ke-Tê-Shu-Yüan private-printed blocks preserved ed.
先緒乙未年刻 毛邊紙
Dated — Kuang-Hsü "Mao Pien" paper
"I-Wei" 21/1895

Index

Bound in 1 tao, 2 chuan (上, 下), 2 ts'ê

Remarks

359

The University of Toronto Chinese Library

. . . .

Accession No. 2151   Index No. 067-ʒ ʌ ʒ b

Title 文萃十三種 Wên Tsui Shih San Chung

Classification C-338

Subject

References

Author 清 張道緒評 Ching. Chang Tao Hsu
                    Commented by

Edition 嘉慶十六年刊 人境軒藏板
        辛未   blocks, preserved,
              Jen. Ching. Hsüan private printed

        Dated — Chia — Ching "Hsin — Wei" 16/1811

Index

Bound in 2 t'áo   20 ts'ê

Remarks

360

The University of Toronto Chinese Library
....

Accession No. 2152 A-B.　　Index No. 102-793²
085-ʒ₂c9

Title 畿輔水利議(附車傳)滇軺紀程(附荷戈紀程)
Chi Fu Shuei Li I (Fu Pêng Chuan), Tien Chao Chi Chêng (Fu Ho Ko
Chi Chêng)　Yao

Classification B—197

Subject

References

Author 清．林則徐進呈稿　Presented to the throne by
Ching. Lin Tsê·Hsü

Edition 家藏版，光緒丙子年刊　連史紙
Private Home Family Edition, dated Kuang·Hsü "Pin·Tzŭ" nien "Lien·shih" paper
1876

Index

Bound in 1 t₅ₐ₀, 2 t₅₂

Remarks

The University of Toronto Chinese Library

. . . .

Accession No. 2153   Index No. 021-cmi

Title 北學編 Pei Hsüeh Pien

Classification 乙 — 308 魏蓮 — 朝七

Subject Miscellaneous writings about the famous
writers scholars since "Han" (漢朝) dynasty
to "Ching" (清朝) dynasty.

References

Author 清魏 蓮陸輯 Collated by ching. Wei Lien-Lu

Edition 連池書院刊, 同治七年刊, 也也輯
Lien-Chih-Shu-Yüan edition, dated Tung-Chih 7/1868

Index a general table of contents for 4 Chüan

Bound in 1 t'ao, 4 Chüan, 附補遺 1 Chüan   3 t'ia
                    attached with "Pu-I" is attached
Remarks

The University of Toronto Chinese Library

. . . .

Accession No. 2154   Index No. 203-dkd

Title 默盦集 Mo An Chi

Classification D — 43

Subject

References

Author 清, 王舟瑤 撰, Written by Ch'ing, Wang Chou-Yao

Edition 上海國光書局, 鉛印本, 有光洋紙 a kind of imported paper Shanghai, Kuo-Kuang Book Company. Kuokuang' Type-setting edition

Index

Bound in 1 t'ao, 3 ts'e

Remarks

363

The University of Toronto Chinese Library

....

Accession No. 2155   Index No. 030-c7eb

Title 合刻延平四先生年譜 Ho Kó Yen ~~Nien~~ Ping Ssŭ ~~Hʃ~~ Hsien
                                    Shêng Nien Pú

Classification B—117

Subject

References

Author 清, 毛念恃訂 Ching. Mao Nien-Chih bound edition

Edition 家藏版，乾隆十年刻年. 綿連紙
        Private~~Hon~~ family edition, Dated Chien-Lung 10/1745.   Mien-Lien~ Paper

Index

Bound in 1 t̆ʒo, 2 t̆s̆e

Remarks

Accession No. 2156   Index No. 120·djPj

Title 素園叢彙 *Su Yüan Ts'ung Kao*

Classification D — 43 引集文

Subject *a collection of writings and discussions of Classics.*

References

Author 清 姚永樸選 *Ch'ing, Yao Yung·Pu* — *Written & Selected by*

Edition 商務印書局石印, 綿連紙
Ching·Wu·Yin·Shu·Chü Lithographic edition, "Mien·Lien" paper

Index *No index*

Bound in *1 t'ao, 2 ts'ê*

Remarks

The University of Toronto Chinese Library

. . . .

Accession No. 2157   Index No. 001-ddgb

Title 世界海軍現狀 Shih Chieh Hai Chün Hsien Chuang

Classification B-297

Subject

References

Author 丁士源 (清), Ching; Ting Shih-Yüan

Edition

Index

Bound in 1 tao, 1 tś'e

Remarks

The University of Toronto Chinese Library

. . . .

Accession No. 2158   Index No. 085-ihgi

Title 溫公家範 Wên Kung Chia Fan

Classification C—13 儒家

Subject

References

Author 清, 朱軾 校正 Ching, Chu Shih.

Edition 家藏版, 毛方紙
Private/family edition, "Mao-Tai" paper

Index No index

Bound in 1 t'ao, 2 ts'ê

Remarks

The University of Toronto Chinese Library

· ·

Accession No. 2159   Index No. 018-mggz

Title 劉海峰文 Liu Hai Fêng Wên

Classification C

Subject

References

Author 清劉大櫆著 Ch'ing, Liu Ta K'uei

Edition 家藏版 Private. printed family edition

Index

Bound in 十卷附詩大卷六冊
10 Chüan

Remarks 同治甲戌年刻
白紙
White paper

368

The University of Toronto Chinese Library

. . . .

Accession No. 2160   Index No. 030- i j e g

Title 單縣周氏家集 Shan Hsien Chou Shih Chia Chi

Classification D

Subject

References

Author 清周鳴鑾著 Ch'ing, Chou Ming Luan

Edition 仿宋精刊本 Fang Sung Fine printed edition

Index

Bound in 二冊   2 Ts'e

Remarks 綿連紙 Mien Lien paper

The University of Toronto Chinese Library

. . . .

13

Accession No. 2161 (A) (B)   Index No. 039-39dk
                                              085-46dk

Title   子夏易傳 Tzü Hsia I Chuan
        漢上易傳 Han Shang I Chuan

Classification A-11

Subject

References

Author 清 朱震集傳 Collected Commentaries by Ching, Chu Chên

Edition 通志堂經解本 Tung Chih Tang (Ching Chieh Pên)
         廣東書局刊   毛邊紙
         Canton book company published Mao Pien-paper

Index

Bound in 1 t'ao   4 chuan each   3 ts'ê

Remarks

370

The University of Toronto Chinese Library

· ·

Accession No. 2162   Index No. 026-ddeg

Title 印光法師文鈔 Yin Kuang Fa Shih Wên Chao

Classification C-513

Subject

References

Author 印光法師著作 Yin-Kuang Fa Shih

Edition

Index

Bound in

Remarks One tao is found on shelf. (two Tsê) According to the table of content there should be 4 Tsê.

After Inventory, both volumes are found May 17, 2007

371

The University of Toronto Chinese Library

· ·

Accession No. 43 2163   Index No. 075/ 33 k b

Title 栗恭勤公年譜 Li Kung Chin Kung Nien Pu

Classification B-107

Subject

References

Author 清 張壬林編輯 edited & compiled by Ching, Chang Jen-Lin

Edition 家藏版 Private printed family edition
光緒年刻　白紙

Index Dated — Kuang-Hsü White paper period 1875—1908

Bound in 1 t'ao 2 ts'ê

Remarks

Accession No. 2164   Index No. 040- 039-ch

Title 字錄 Tzŭ Lu

Classification c-13

Subject

References

Author 李調元撰 Written by Li T'iao-Yüan

Edition

Index

Bound in 1 tao   2 ts'è

Remarks

The University of Toronto Chinese Library

. . . .

Accession No. 2165   Index No. 009-nZ²9

Title 儒门法语 Ju Mên Fa Yü

Classification C—13 儒学

Subject a collection of commentaries on philosophy, and classics.

References

Author 清, 彭定求辰阳撰 originally edited by Ching, Pêng Ting-Chiu

Edition 小果斋句章刊 彭氏刻本, 乾隆卅五年, 竹紙板 Pêng-Shih block-printing edition, dated Chien-Lung 35/1770
Bamboo paper

Index None

Bound in 1 t₀, a thê

Remarks

The University of Toronto Chinese Library

· ·

Accession No. 2166   Index No. 120-dbb3

Title 池蕭古文鈔 *Chún Pú Ku Wên Cháo*

Classification D — 43-別集一文

Subject an individual collection of prose

References

Author 清, 戴梓湮, written by *Chíng, Tai Chi*

Edition 家藏版, 同治庚午年刊 朱連紙

Private family edition, dated *Tùng-Chih Kêng-Wu* / 1870
"*Chia-Lien*" Paper

Index none

Bound in 1 函, 6 *chüan*, 2 *t'sê*

Remarks

The University of Toronto Chinese Library

. . . .

Accession No. 2167   Index No. 064- 89bi

Title 拾餘四种 Shih Yü Ssŭ Chung

Classification C 308 雜家 — 雜文 (full miscellaneous
Tsa Chia   Tsa Wên   writings)

Subject miscellaneous writings

References

Author 清, 刘沅楳 Ching, Liu Yüan

Edition 私家版, 光绪年刻, 毛边纸 (1875-1908)
Private family Edition, dated Kuang-Hsü period, Mao-Pien paper

Index None

Bound in 1 t'ao, 2 chüan, 2 tsê

Remarks

376

The University of Toronto Chinese Library

. . . .

Accession No. 2168   Index No. 073-788i

Title 書目長編 Shu Mu Chʻang Pien

Classification B—337 目錄

Subject a general catalogues

References

Author 清, 即 邵瑞彭等輯 Compiled by Chʻing, Shao Jui-Pʻêng and others

Edition 鉛印本, 津白毛邊紙 Type-setting edition, Western imported White "Mao-Pien" Paper

Index a general table of contents for 2 chüan

Bound in / tʻao, 2 chüan, 2 tsê

Remarks

The University of Toronto Chinese Library

. . . .

Accession No. 2169   Index No. 053-ㄏㄨㄚㄨ

Title 康熙幾暇格物編 Káng Hsi Chi Hsia Ko Wu Pien

Classification C — 308 朝方 — 朝大
                    348 教主.

Subject

References

Author 清康熙帝御撰 Written by Ching, Káng-Hsi Emperor

Edition 房寿石印, 清代 imported
        Manuscript, Lithographic, Western paper

Index none

Bound in 1 tȧo. 6 chüan, 2 tsȇ

Remarks

The University of Toronto Chinese Library

. . . .

Accession No. 2170   Index No. 030-cc7k

Title 名法指掌 Ming Fa Chih Chang

Classification B302

Subject

References

Author

Edition 道光四年增訂 粵東刊板
                    Yüeh-Tung ed. engraved blocks
          Dated — Tao-Kuang "Chia-Shen" 4/1824

Index

Bound in 1 tao, 4 ts'è

Remarks

The University of Toronto Chinese Library

. . . .

Accession No. 2171   Index No. 085-33dev

Title 水流雲在龕梟詩存 Shui Liu Yün Tsai Kuan Chi
                                      Shi Tsun

Classification D — 38 51集 一詩

Subject an individual collection of poetry

References

                                      Collated by
Author 清周天麟纂, Ching, Chou Tien-Lin

Edition 仿西法石印 光绪十七年印, 粉纸
         Imitated Western   lithographic edition,
         powder   ^ dated Kuang-Hsü 17/1891
         "fên" paper

Index none

Bound in / tbo, 2 tsê

Remarks

The University of Toronto Chinese Library

....

Accession No. 2172 Index No. 002-Czme

Title 中日議和紀略 Chung Jih I Ho Chi Lüeh

Classification B—32 紀事本末

Subject a historical narratives of the China-Japan treaty in Kwang-Hsu 21年

References

Author

Edition 活字版，綿連紙

Movable type edition, "Mien-Lien" paper

Index none

Bound in 1 tao, 2 tsê

Remarks

The University of Toronto Chinese Library

. . . .

Accession No. 2173   Index No. 140-ii c 7

Title 抱晷軒詩文集 Pao Yü Hsüan Shih Wên Chi

Classification D—33 別集—清代

Subject *an individual collection of prose and poetry.*

References

Author 清, 其啟璜 *Written by* Ching, Ying Chi

Edition 家藏板, 光緒年刊, 連史紙
Private Family Home Edition, dated Kuang-Hsü period (1875-1908)
"Lien-shih" paper

Index *none*

Bound in / *tao, 2 chüan, 2 ts'ê*

Remarks

The University of Toronto Chinese Library

....

Accession No. 2174   Index No. 077-33 C ?

Title 止止軒詩稿 Chih Chih Hsüan Shih Kao

Classification D-38

Subject

References

Author 清 趙鈞著 Ching, Chao Chün

Edition 甲子年重刻 Re-engraved in "Chia-Tzu" Period.

Index

Bound in 1 t'ao 4 ts'e

Remarks

Accession No. 2135   Index No. 120-n3

Title 駢珠 Pien Chu

Classification ㄷ一258 譜錄

Subject natural science

References

Author 隋杜公瞻撰 Written by Suei, Tu Kung-Chan

Edition 官刻本 康熙37年刻, 綿連紙
official-printed edition, dated Kang-Hsi 37/1698, "Mien-Lien" paper

Index a general table of contents for 4 chüan

Bound in 1 t'ao, 4 chüan, 續 2 chüan, 2 ts'e
Hsü

Remarks

The University of Toronto Chinese Library

· ·

Accession No. 2176   Index No. 031.b3°89

Title 四書朋澹集叶 Ssŭ Shu Chêng Yü Chi Tui

Classification A—131—四書

Subject a collection of

References

Author 清, 楊瑜快棋 Compiled by Ching, Chieh Yü-Chên

Edition 昭世室藏板
        Chao-Jang. Tang edition blocks preserved.

Index none

Bound in 1 套, 2 册

Remarks

....

Accession No. 2178　　　　Index No. 120-0bze

Title 續古文苑 Hsü Ku Wēn Yuan

Classification δ

Subject

References

Author 清孫星衍選 Selected by: Ch'ing, Sun Hsing Yen

Edition 江蘇書局版 Printed by Chiang Su Books Co.

Index

Bound in 二十卷六四 20 Chuan 6 Tsê

Remarks 光緒年刻 Block-engraving in "Kuang Hsü" Period.
連史紙 Lien-Shih paper
夾板 Wooden folder

387

The University of Toronto Chinese Library

. . . .

Accession No. 2180   Index No. 040-3213

Title 宣和譜牙牌彙集 Hsüan Ho Pu Ya Pai Hui Chi

Classification C—238 藝術—雜技

Subject a special kind of Chinese chess game

References

Author 浪槐河上漁人杏園韓, 博昌教人雪庵氏重訂
Compiled by Lang-Huai-Ho Shang, Yü Jên, Hsing Yüan (韓), Po-Chang-San-Jen, Yün-
                                                                    An-Shih revised.
Edition 家藏版. 光緒年刻, 揉連紙版
        Private family edition, dated Kuang-Hsü period, "Hsüan-Lien" paper
                                                (1875-1908)

Index a general table of contents for two chüan

Bound in 1 tao, 2 tsê, 2 chüan.

Remarks

Accession No. 2181   Index No. 075-hijc

Title 棗強縣志補正 Tsao Chiang Hsien Chih Pu Chêng

Classification B 194

Subject

References

Author 清 方宗誠篡 Compiled by Ch'ing, Fang Tsung-Chêng

Edition 同治十二年刊
Dated — Tung-Chih "Kuei-Yu" 12/1873

Index

Bound in 1 tao

Remarks

389

The University of Toronto Chinese Library

. . . .

Accession No. 2182   Index No. 077-n z e a

Title 歸方評點史記合筆 Kuei Fang P'ing Tien Shih Chi Hê Pi

Classification B

Subject

References

Author 明歸有光 清方苞評點 ~~Conf~~ Commented & punctuated by Ming. Kuei Yu Kuang & Ching Fang Pao.

Edition 望三益齋刊本 Wang San I Chai Block-printing edition

Index

Bound in 六卷四冊 6 Chuan 4 Ts'ê

Remarks 綿連紙 Mien-Lien paper
夾板 wooden-folder

390

The University of Toronto Chinese Library

．．．．．．．．．．．．．．．．．．．．．．．．

Accession No. 2184   Index No. 030-bbmp

Title 古今學變   Ku Chin Hsüeh Pien

Classification 乙──13 傳記

Subject a collection of commentaries on the change
of old philosophy.

References

Author 日本 伊藤長胤山春   Japan, I Têng Chǎng-Yin

Edition 皇都書林 林權兵衛對山板   店師版、大楷
Huang-Tu Shu-Lin, Lin-Chüan-Ping-Wei
Korean paper, wooden block folder

Index a general table of contents for 3 chüan

Bound in 1 t̆ŏ, 3 chüan, 3 tsè

Remarks

The University of Toronto Chinese Library

. . . .

Accession No. 2185   Index No. 169-ddと

Title 閑邪錄 Hsien Hsieh Lu

Classification と一308 報告一報文

Subject *Miscellaneous writings and discussions about the "good & evil".*

References

Author 清姚瑞修公居奏 蔣正枕補輯
Originally compiled by, Ching, Yao Tuan-Loo [Chieh] Kung, Chiang Chêng-Hsiao revised

Edition 三經堂藏板, 乾隆年刻 白紙
Block preserved ³San-Chien-Tâng edition, dated Chien Lung period (1736-1795) white paper

Index *a general table of contents for 10 Chüan*

Bound in *1 t'ao, 10 chüan, 2 ts'e*

Remarks

The University of Toronto Chinese Library
....

Accession No. 2186   Index No. 108- 2天天

Title 益智圖 I Chih Tú

Classification C—238 藝術 一 親扶

Subject miscellaneous arts and crafts, and games

References

Author 清, 童叶庚著, Ching, Túng Hsieh-Kêng

Edition 京都琉璃廠寶構玉宝齋牧, 張建修 block preserved
Ching-Tu, Liu-Li-Chang, Chüng-Lin-Shu-Shih edition edition
"Mien-'Lien" paper

Index a general table of contents for 2 tsè.

Bound in 1 tè. 2 tsè

Remarks

393

. . . .

18

<u>Accession No.</u> 2188   <u>Index No.</u> ~~055-azbl 077-zzzb~~ 061-dzbl

<u>Title</u> 念一史彈詞註 *Nien I Shih Tán Tzŭ Chu*

<u>Classification</u> ~~B-52~~ D-38 別集 — 詩

<u>Subject</u> - (Gest No. 2962) "a very brief synopsis of Chinese history in verse; the period covered being from the earliest times down to the close of the Yüan Dynasty." This item includes the Ming Dynasty.

<u>References</u> -012- zafk 16/22   ~~Gest No. 2962~~, Toronto Nos 862, 1033, 1146

<u>Author</u> 明 楊慎纂。 Written by *Ming, Yang Shên*

<u>Edition</u> 珍瓏山館藏版 *Ling-Lung-Shan-Kuan* ~~press printed~~ block-preserved ed.
乾隆年刻 毛邊紙 鐵嶺鍾氏藏
"Mao Pien" paper   Teh-Ling & Chung-Shih

<u>Index</u> *Dated — Chien-Lung period 1736 - 1795*

<u>Bound in</u> 1 t'ao   2 ts'ê

<u>Remarks</u> *synopsis*

394

The University of Toronto Chinese Library
....

Accession No. 仔 2190   Index No. 044-e3ie

Title 屈子楚词章句 Chü Tzŭ Chu Tzŭ Chang Chü

Classification D—14 楚辭

Subject Elegies of "Chu"

References

Author 清, 刘梦鹏著 Ching, Liu Mêng-Péng

Edition 藜青堂版, 嘉庆五年刻, 白纸
Li-Ching-Tang edition, dated Chia-Ching 5/1800
white paper

Index A general table of contents for each chüan

Bound in 1 t'ao, 7 chüan, 3 t'sê

Remarks

Accession No. 2191   Index No. 030·dzzi

Title 呂氏十種叢書 Lü Shih Shih Chung Tsung Shu

Classification c-338

Subject

References

Author 明 呂坤著 Ming, Lü Kun

Edition 清康熙年間重刊
        Dated — Ching, K'ang-Hsi period 1662–1722 printed edition
                                              re-printed

Index

Bound in

Remarks

The University of Toronto Chinese Library

....

Accession No. 2192   Index No. 162/ynkz

Title 通鑑綱目前言 T'ung Chien Kang Mu Yün Yen

Classification ß 一 22 偏年

Subject annals; with commentary

References

Author 清, 柯曉凮著 Ching, Ko Hsiao-Kang

Edition 問心堂藏版 康熙年刋, 毛邊紙
Wên-Hsin+-T'ang edition, 'blocks preserved' Kang-Hsi period (1662-1722)
"Mao-Pien" paper

Index a general chronological list of contents
for 2 the

Bound in 1 t'ho, 2 t'se

Remarks

397

Accession No. 2193   Index No. 131-k390

Title 臨文便覽 Lin Wên Pien Lan

Classification A — 151 小學

Subject *Phonetic*
Phonographical and graphic dictionaries

References

Author 清, 彭翰唐壽楊等 (Written by) Ching. Lung Han-Chên and others

Edition 松林齋刊, 光緒年刻, 粉印
Sung-Lin-Chai edition, dated Kuang-Hsü period (1875-1908),
"Fên" paper

Index
none

Bound in 1 tào, 2 tsê

Remarks

The University of Toronto Chinese Library

· ·

₈

Accession No. 2194   Index No. 060-1dgd

Title 徵君孫先生年譜 附遊譜中州人物考
Cheng Hui Chün Sun Hsien Shêng Nien Pú
Classification B-107   Fu Yu Pú Chung chou Jen Wu Káo

Subject

References

Author 明 孫奇逢 清 湯斌 編次
Edited by Ming, Sun Chi-Fêng; Ching, Tang Pin
Edition 懷遠堂梓 Huai-Yüan-Táng
康熙壬寅年刻 綿連紙
"Mien Lien" paper
Index Dated — Kàng-Hsi "Jên-Ying" 1/1662

Bound in 1 tao, 4 ts'ê, 2 chuan (年譜 2 chuan, 遊譜 1 chuan)

Remarks

Accession No. 2195   Index No. 061-K339

Title 慶典章程 Ching Tien Kêng Chang Chêng

Classification B-287

Subject

References

Author

Edition 清乾隆內務府,禮部,工部諭批彙章
Ching, Chien-Lung Nei Wu Fu, Li Pu, Kung Pu

Index

Bound in 1 tao, 5 ts'ê

Remarks

The University of Toronto Chinese Library

. . . .

Accession No. 2196   Index No. 140·ggl

Title 英法俄德四國志略 Yin Fa O Tê Ssŭ Kuo Chih Lüeh

Classification B 227

Subject

References

Author 沈敦和輯譯。 *Compiled & Translated by* Shên Tun-Ho

Edition 光緒十八年四月周隹 *Dated — Kuang-Hsü "Jên-Chên" 18/1892 April*

Index

Bound in 1 tao, 2 ts'ê

Remarks

401

The University of Toronto Chinese Library
....

Accession No. 2197   Index No. 061-ᴣ ᴣ88

Title 怡情書室詩鈔 I Ching Shu Shih Shih Chao

Classification D-38

Subject

References

Author 清 睿恪親王著 Ching, Jun-Ko Chin Wang

Edition 乾隆己酉新鐫
Dated — Chien-Kung "Chi-Yu" 54/1789

Index

Bound in 1 táo 1 tsé

Remarks

The University of Toronto Chinese Library

. . . .

Accession No. 2199 A-B   Index No. 037-去大
                                          064-尺人

Title
A. 奏摺對 B. 摺譜 A. Tsou Tui   B. Chê Pú

Classification
         B-72 詔令奏議——奏議

Subject

References

Author   A. 傳受播珠王洪承疇 清 A. Hung chêng-chou
                                        ching
         B. 謨章, 饒句宣嵇生纂 B. Yü Chang, Yao Hsün-Hsüan (Sung-Shêng)
                              compiled by

Edition   A. 京都二酉齋藏版, 光緒庚寅仲秋刊, 琉璃廠書局.
          Ching-Tu, Êrh-Yu-Chai, edition, dated Kuang-Hsü "Kêng Yin"   block preserved   /1890
          Liu-Li-Chang Book Company printed.   autumn

Index   A. none
          B. A general table of content of 1 chüan

Bound in A. 1 tsê, 2 chüan

Remarks   B. 1 tsê, 1 chüan

403

The University of Toronto Chinese Library

. . . .

Accession No. 2200   Index No. 061-ЛеС4

Title 惜抱軒集 Hsi Pao Hsüan Chi

Classification D-43

Subject

References

Author 清 姚鼐 著 Ching, Yao Nai

Edition

Index

Bound in 1 t'ao 8 ts'ê

Remarks

The University of Toronto Chinese Library
....

12

Accession No. 2201   Index No. 120·gjdc

Title 經韻集字析解 *Ching Yün Chi Tzŭ Hsi Chieh*

Classification A-116

Subject

References

Author 清 彭良敞集註 *Ching, Pêng Liang-Chʻang* (Collected & annotated)

Edition 長臻重刊本 *Chʻang-Chên* ~~second ed.~~ (reprinted edition by)

綿連紙 *"Mien Lien" paper.*

Index

Bound in 1 tʻao, 2 chuan, 4 tsʻê

Remarks

The University of Toronto Chinese Library

. . . .

Accession No. 2202   Index No. 114 - d 罗诗

Title 禺山雜著 Yü Shan Tsa Chu

Classification D—38 別集 一 詩 (Individual collection =
                          Pieh chi   Shih   poetry)

Subject an individual collection of prose poetry with
commentary & pictures.

References

Author 清, 李楊著 Ching, Li Yang

Edition 另藏板, 竹紙本
Private family Home edition, Bamboo paper

Index a general table of contents for 4 tsè

Bound in 1 t'ao, 3 kinds, 4 tsè

Remarks

The University of Toronto Chinese Library

· ·

Accession No. *2206*   Index No. *167-3dab*

Title 金忠節公文集 *Chin Chung Chieh Kung Wên Chi*

Classification *D-23*

Subject

.

References

Author 明 金聲著 *Ming, Chin Shêng*

Edition 道光丁亥鐫
Dated — Tao-Kuang "Ting-Hai" 7/1827

Index

Bound in *1 táo. 4 tsʻê*

Remarks

The University of Toronto Chinese Library

. . . .

Accession No. 2207   Index No. 001-abbz

Title   七召六畫圖 Chi Chiao Liu Shu Tú

Classification   C-238

Subject

References

Author   清,毛應觀著 Ching, Mao Yin-Kuang

Edition   家藏版   竹纸
Private family edition   Bamboo Paper

Index   A general index of all the characters names of the diagrams

Bound in   1 tsé, 1 táo

Remarks

The University of Toronto Chinese Library

. . . .

Accession No. 2218   Index No. 031-b点d♀

Title 四聲易知錄 Ssǔ Shêng I Chih Lu

Classification A——166 小學一韻書

Subject *Phonetic dictionary*

References

Author 清 姚文田 *Compiled by* Ching, Yao Wên-Tien

Edition 廣州修補印行, 光緒八年印, 綿連紙
Kuang-Chou Hsiu-Pu printed, dated Kuang-Hsü 8/1882,
"Mien-Lien" paper

Index *a general table of contents for 4 chüan*

Bound in *1 táo, 4 chüan, 2 tsê*

Remarks

The University of Toronto Chinese Library

. . . .

Accession No. 2210   Index No. 042-3m

Title 小學, 附考傳 Hsiao Hsüeh Fu Hsiao Chuan

Classification A—151 V. 3

Subject

References

Author 宋, 朱熹 著, 長洲彭定求 訂源泰

Edition 附考傳 — 晉 陶潛書
Sung, Chu Hsi (著) compiled by Chang-Chou, Pêng-Ting, Chin Fang-Lien (集)
"Hsiao-Chuan" — Chin, Tao Chien (著)

Index none

Bound in 1 Tao, 2 Chüan, 2 Tsê with

Remarks

The University of Toronto Chinese Library

. . . .

4

Accession No. Z 211   Index No. 051-bekp

Title 平定關隴紀略 Ping Ting Kuan Lung Chi Lüeh

Classification B-32

Subject

References

Author 清 易孔昭纂輯 Compiled by Ching. I Kung-Chao

Edition 蘭州署藏版 Block preserved in Lan-Chou-Shu private printed

光緒年刊　綿連紙

Index Dated — Kuang-Hsü "Mien Lien" paper period 1875 — 1908

Bound in 2 tao   13 chuan   12 ts'e

Remarks

The University of Toronto Chinese Library

. . . .

Accession No. 2212   Index No. 075-Ki上b

Title 箬匋室古匹體詩 Lo Tao Tang Ku Chin Ti Shih

Classification D — 38 31體 — 詩

Subject an individual collection of poetry.

References

Author 袭蕤工蕤 ching, Kung-Chin-Wang

Edition 同治六年 丁卯新 dated Tung Chih 6/1867

Index none

Bound in 1 t'ao, 2 chüan, 2 ts'e

Remarks

Accession No. 2214   Index No. 140-79hp

Title 茹經堂叢書 Ju Ching Tang Tsung Shu

Classification C-338

Subject

References

Author 唐文治著,輯,及其演講稿 Compiled by Tang Wên-Chih

Edition

Index

Bound in 8 tao 31 tsʼe

Remarks

The University of Toronto Chinese Library

．．．．．．．．．．．．．．．．．．．．．．．．

Accession No. 2215   Index No. 085-9c88

Title 涉江詩稿,遺稿 Shê Chiang Shih Kao, I Kao

Classification D—33-刽第一詩文

Subject An individual collection of poetry & prose

References

Author 清,唐鼋蓉. / Ching, Tang Yen

Edition 鉛印本 毛四低
　　　　　　　　edition,
Type-setting ∧ "Mao-Pien" paper

Index None

Bound in / 40. 卷 / 册

Remarks

414

The University of Toronto Chinese Library

. . . .

Accession No. 2216   Index No. 167-h l g o

Title 錢遵王讀書敏求記校證
Ch'ien Tsun Wang Tu Shu Min Chiu Chi Chiao Cheng

Classification C-308

Subject

References

Author 清管庭芬等 Ch'ing, Kuan Ting Fen + others

Edition 長州韋氏刊 Chang-Chou, Chang Shih

Index

Bound in 九卷六册 9 Chuan 6 Tsê

Remarks 民國丙寅出版 ~~Polish~~ Published in "Ping Yin" of the
連史紙 Lien-Shih Paper   Republic.

415

The University of Toronto Chinese Library
. . . .

Accession No. 2217   Index No. 172-9zic

Title (明) 虫 鳴寉存人牘 Shuang Yü Ou Tsun Chih Tu
雙

Classification D—43 丸/年—文

Subject an individual collection of prose — letters

References

Author 清 朱穎莘 Ching, Chu Ying

Edition 凸藤板, 乾隆年刊, 竹紙

Private family edition, dated Chien-Lung period, (1736-1795)
        Bamboo paper

Index a separate table of content for each chüan

Bound in 1 t8°, 2 t8°, 2 chüan

Remarks

416

The University of Toronto Chinese Library
....

Accession No. 2218   Index No. 005-bed

Title 也是集 Yeh Shih Chi

Classification D — 4331 華文

Subject an individual collection of prose

References

Author 清, 葉華葊 Ching, Ying Hua

Edition 鉛印本, 油光紙,
a kind of imported paper.
Type-setting edition "Yu-Kuang" Paper

Index None

Bound in 1 t'ao, 2 t'sê, 附許篇
attached with "Hsü Pien"

Remarks

The University of Toronto Chinese Library
....

Accession No. 2219.   Index No. 053-2d2g

Title 廣雅堂詩集 Kuang Ya Tang Shih Chi

Classification D—38 別集一 詩

Subject an individual collection of poetry

References

Author 清, 南皮 張之洞著, Ching, Chang Chih-Tung

Edition 石印本, 江史紙 a kind of imported paper.
Lithographic edition, "Yu-Kuang" paper

Index None

Bound in 1 t'ao, 2 chüan, 2 ts'e

Remarks

The University of Toronto Chinese Library

· ·

Accession No. 2220   Index No. 057· 上3太太

Title 張文襄幕府紀聞 Chang Wên Hsiang Mu Fu Chi Wên

Classification 乙－308 雜文

Subject Miscellaneous Writings

References

Author 清漢濱漱爲辜撰 (Written by) Ching. Han Pin Tu I Chê

Edition 活字版, 大字本. 宣統庚戌十刻. 辟建亦
Movable-type edition, big characters, dated Hsüan-Tüng Kêng-Hsü /1910.
"Mien-Lien" paper Cotton paper sized with alum.

Index a general table of contents for 2 t'sê

Bound in 1 t'ao, 2 t'sê

Remarks

419

The University of Toronto Chinese Library

....

Accession No. *2222*   Index No. *180-JP*

Title 韻籟 *Yün Lai*

Classification *A — 166* 小學 — 韻書

Subject *Phonetic dictionary*

References

Author 清．華長忠著 *Ching, Hua Chang-Chung*

Edition 松竹齋版，左[?]書[?]刻，近[?]代
   Sung-Chu-Chai edition, dated Kuang-Hsü period (1875-1908)

Index *A general table of the words classified in different tunes*

Bound in *1 t'ao, 4 chüan, 2 t'ie*

Remarks

The University of Toronto Chinese Library

....

Accession No. 2223   Index No. 060-hhri

Title 御製勸善要言 Yü Chih Chüan Shan Yao Yen

Classification C —— 308 桃告 一批文

Subject miscellaneous ~~entry of the~~ teachings of good personality 漢文, 四文 好好
        With both "Han-Wen" and "Hui-Wen"

References

Author

Edition 敕版, 滿漢文合刊, 連史紙
        Palace edition, Man Han Wen printed together, "Lien-Shih" paper

Index none

Bound in 1 t'ao, 1 t'ai

Remarks

421

The University of Toronto Chinese Library

. . . .

Accession No. 2225   Index No. 189-3b3d

Title 高上玉皇本行集經 Kao Shang Yü Huang Pên Hsing Chi Ching

Classification C-513

Subject

References

Author 清 張煦奉旨抄寫 Ching, Chang Chao (manuscript)

Edition 乾隆二年 殿本 Palace ed.
Dated — Chien-Lung "Ting-Ssū" 2/1037

Index

Bound in 1 t'ao   3 ts'ê

Remarks

422

The University of Toronto Chinese Library

. . . .

Accession No. 2226   Index No. 032-2gh

Title 墨餘錄 Mo Yü Lu

Classification E—308 雜品 — 雜文

Subject miscellaneous writings ; with commentary

References

Author 清, 毛祥麟著 Ching, Mao Kui-Shan

Edition 文元堂版, 毛太紙
        Wên-Yüan-Tang edition, "Mao-Tai" paper

Index a general table of contents for 16 Chüan

Bound in 1 t'ao, 16 Chüan, 6 t'sê

Remarks

423

The University of Toronto Chinese Library

. . . .

3

Accession No. 2228   Index No. 001-bmk

Title 三禮圖 San Li Tú

Classification A-61

Subject

References

Author 宋 聶崇義輯註 Compiled & Annotated by Sung, Nieh Chúng-I

Edition 上海同文書局石印本 Shanghai, Túng-Wén book company lithographic ed.
連史紙
"Lien Shih" paper

Index

Bound in 1 tao, 20 chuan, 20 tsǎ

Remarks

24

Accession No. 2229   Index No. 118-33cc

Title 竹書紀年校正 *Chu Shu Chi Nien Hsiao Chêng*

Classification B-22

Subject

References

Author 梁 沈約附注 *Liang, Shên+ Yüeh to place with the record.*

Edition 東路廳署刊 *Tung-Lu-Ting-Shu published*
光緒五年刻 竹紙
己卯
Bamboo paper
Index *Dated — Kuang-Hsü "Chi-Mao" 5/1879*

Bound in 1 t'ao   14 chuan   2 ts'ǔ

Remarks

425

The University of Toronto Chinese Library

. . . .

Accession No. 2230   Index No. 031. m g l g

Title 圜悟禪師碧巖集   Huan Wu Ch'an Shih Pi Yen Chi

Classification C-5-13

Subject

References

Author 秣陵遠庵吳自牧 校 天界比丘性湛閱   Tien Chieh Pi Chiu Hsin Chan

Collated by Mo Ling Yüan An, Wu Tzŭ-Hung

Edition 清光緒二年比丘開慧募資重刻   杭州熙慶寺慧空經房存板

Re-engraved by Pi Chiu Kai Hui Mu Tzŭ reprinted

Hang Chou Chao-Ching-Ssŭ, Hui-Kung Ching fang private ed.

Index Dated — Ch'ing, Kuang-Hsü "Ping-Tzŭ" 2/1876

Bound in 1 t'ao 5 tsê

Remarks

426

The University of Toronto Chinese Library

．．．．．．．．．．．．．．．．．．．．．．．．

Accession No. 2232   Index No. 040-k3d

Title 定盦文集 Ting An Wên Chi

Classification D-43

Subject

References

Author 嬾 龔自珍著 Kung Tzŭ-Chên

Edition 清光緒丁酉年萬本書堂校刊) 粵東金經閣藏板
Wan-Pên-Shu-Tang. revised ed. Block preserved in
Yüeh Tung Chin-Ching Ko
privite printed
Dated — Ching, Kuang-Hsü "Ting-Yu" 23/1897

Index

Bound in 1 táo 6 tsě

Remarks

427

Accession No. 2234   Index No. 212-gegb

Title 龍泉師友遺稿合編 Lung Ch'üan Shih Yu I Kao Hê Pien

Classification

Subject

References

Author 清王晉之等撰 *Written by* Ch'ing, Wang Chin Chih & others

Edition 家藏版 Private-*family* Printed ed.

Index

Bound in 十三卷六冊 13 Chuan 6 Tsê

Remarks 光緒二十三年刊
竹紙 Bamboo paper

428

The University of Toronto Chinese Library

. . . .

Accession No. 2235   Index No. 106-3379

40

Title 白鹿書院志, Pai Pai Lu Shu Yüan Chih

Classification 3 - 217

Subject

References

Author 星子縣知縣毛德琦原訂, Originally founded edition by Hsing Tzü Hsien Chih Hsien Mao Te-chi;
署南康府事周兆蘭重修 Shu Nan Kang Fu Shih Chou Chao Lan (revised)

Edition 同治十年補刊
Dated — Tung-chih "Hsin-Wei" 10/1871

Index

Bound in 1 tao, 19 chuan, 8 ts'ê

Remarks

The University of Toronto Chinese Library

. . . .

Accession No. 2236   Index No. 030-9387

Title 唐子潛書 Táng Tzǔ Chien Shu

Classification ㄷ—308 雜家—雜文
                        Tsa Chia — Tsa Wên (Miscellaneous
                                                    Writing)
Subject

References

Author 清, 唐甄著 Ching, Táng Chên

Edition 家藏版, 毛邊紙
Private Family   Home edition, "Mao Pien" paper

Index a general table of contents for 4 thê

Bound in 1 t'ao, 4 thê

Remarks

The University of Toronto Chinese Library

· ·

Accession No. *19* 2238   Index No. *181-22c1*

Title 顧閣年譜 *Ku Yen Nien Pu*

Classification *B-107*

Subject

References

Author 清 張穆編 *edited by* *Ching, Chang Mu*

Edition 家藏版 *Privated printed family edition*
道光二十四年刻 綿連紙 *cotton paper sized with alum.*

Index *Dated — Tao-Kuang "Chia-Chen" 24/1844* *"Mien Lien" paper*

Bound in *1 t'ao   2 ts'é*

Remarks

The University of Toronto Chinese Library

....

Accession No. 2239   Index No. 075.3cbc

Title 校刊史記集解索隱正義札記

Hsiao Kàn Shih Chi Chi Chieh So Yin Chèng I Tsa Chi

Classification B. — 12 之 史

Subject Commentaries of "Shih - Chi"

References

Author 清, 張文虎校 Collated by
Ching, Chang Wên-Hu

Edition 金陵書局刊本, 宣紙印, 同治七年甲申本刻)

Chin - Ling Book Company printed, "Kuan-Tui" paper.
Dated Tùng - Chih "jên shên"/1872

Index none

Bound in 1 tào, 5 chüan, 2 tiè

Remarks

432

The University of Toronto Chinese Library

. . . .

Accession No. 2240 ⁵⁹   Index No. 128-gil2

Title 聖諭像解 Shêng Yü Hsiang Chieh

Classification C-13

Subject explanation of the "Sacred Edict" with numerous illustrations of the ancient worthies noted for their good reputation and virtuous conduct.

References Toronto nos. 6, T. 8

Author 梁延年 Liang Yen-nien   承寧堂梓 Chêng-Hsüan-Táng

Edition ~~a reprint by Wên-ching-Táng~~ 味經堂 (title-page) dated ~~Hsien-Fêng~~ "ping-chien" 4/1856 Blocks; "fen" paper

Index 康熙二十年 Dated — Kêng-Hsi "Hsin-Yu" 20/1681

Bound in 2 táo 10 tsɨ

Remarks

433

The University of Toronto Chinese Library

. . . .

Accession No. 2241   Index No. 040-9313

Title 宸垣識略 Chên Yüan Shih Lüeh

Classification B-194 別志.

Subject

References

Author 清 吳太初 輯 Compiled by Ch'ing, Wu T'ai-Ch'u

Edition 池北草堂版 Chih-Pei-Tsao-Tang edition
乾隆年刻 dated Chien-Lung period (1736-1795)

Index 白綿紙 "Pai-Mien" paper

Bound in 1 t'ao 16 chüan 8 ts'e

Remarks

434

The University of Toronto Chinese Library

． ． ． ． ． ． ． ． ． ． ． ． ． ． ． ． ． ． ． ．

Accession No. 2242   Index No. 011-f d d g

Title 雨般秋雨盦隨筆 Liang Pan Ch'iu Yü Cen Sui Pi

Classification c

Subject

References

Author 清梁紹壬纂 Compiled by Ch'ing, Liang Shao Jen.

Edition 振綺堂刊 Cheng I T'ang Block-printing edition

Index

Bound in 八卷八冊 8 Chüan 8 Ts'e

Remarks 道光十七年刻 Block engraving in the 17 year of
粉紙 Powder paper   Tao Kang.

The University of Toronto Chinese Library

....

Accession No. 2244   Index No. 076- LCCH

Title 欽定回疆則 (13.) Chin Ting Hui Chiang Tsê Li

Classification B - 257 釋官

Subject Officials and their duties

References

Author 有, 托津寺奉勒撰 *Written by* Ching. To Chin and others

Edition 活字板排印本 光緒卅四年, 毛邊紙
Movable-type edition, dated Kuang-Hsü 34/1908.
"Mao-Pien" paper

Index None

Bound in 1 t'ao, 8 chüan, 3 tsê

Remarks

436

The University of Toronto Chinese Library

· ·

31

Accession No. 2245   Index No. 067-3888

Title 文獻通考合纂 Wên Hsien Tung Káo Ho Tsüan

Classification B-282

Subject

References

Author 馬端臨著 Ma Tuan-Lin

Edition 沈南湖輯
Compiled by Shên-Nan-Hu

Index

Bound in 1 tao, 4 ts'ê

Remarks

The University of Toronto Chinese Library

· ·

53

Accession No. 2247   Index No. 053-Lzi

Title 庸行編 Yung Hsing Pien

Classification C-308

Subject

References

Author 清 史典原輯 年允中纂補 Originally Compiled by amended edition by
                                         ∧Ching. Shih Tien; ∧Mou Yün-Chung

Edition 康熙卅年刊
        Dated — K'ang-Hsi "Hsin-Wei" 30/1691
        家藏版 Private family/house edition
Index   毛边紙 "Mao-Pien" paper

Bound in 1 t'ao 4 ts'ê

Remarks

The University of Toronto Chinese Library

．．．．．．．．．．．．．．．．．．．．．

Accession No. *2248*   Index No. *128-kccg*

Title　聰訓齋語（附澄懷園語，澄懷主人年譜）
Tsung Hsün Chai Yü (Fu Chêng Huai Yüan Yü, Chêng Huai Chu Jên Nien Pu)

Classification　*c.308*　雜家雜文

Subject

References

Author　張清英著 *Chang Ching-Ying*

Edition

家藏版 *Private family edition*

光緒六年刻 *dated Kuang-Hsü 6/1880*

Index　毛邊紙 *"Mao-Pien" paper*

Bound in　*1 tao　4 chuan*

Remarks　澄懷園語 *4 chuan "Chêng Huai Yüan Yü" 4 chüan*

澄懷主人自訂年譜 *6 chuan "Chêng Huai Chu Jên Ting Nien Pu"
6 chüan*

439

The University of Toronto Chinese Library

....

Accession No. 2249   Index No. 060- lllm

Title 御製繙譯四書 Yü Chih fan I Ssŭ Shu

Classification A-131

Subject

References

Author 乾隆帝御製   鄂文泰鑒定
        Chien-Lung Emperor; O Wên-Tai

Edition 聚珍堂刊 光緒年重刊 竹紙
        Chü Chên-Tang   Bamboo paper
        Dated — Kuang-Hsü period 1895—1908

Index

Bound in 1 t'ao   6 ts'ê

Remarks

. . . .

Accession No. 2250   Index No. 040-lmkl

Title 寫禮廎遺書 四种 Hsieh Li Chin I Chu Ssu Chung

Classification D-33 別集一清代

Subject an individual collection of prose + poetry

References

Author 清. 王頌蔚 Written by 撰 Ching, Wang Sung-Wei

Edition 鄂漢王氏刊 竹紙 Fu-Hsi, Wang Shih edition, Bamboo paper

Index a general table of contents for 4 t'ie

Bound in 1 t'ao, 4 t'ie

Remarks

441

The University of Toronto Chinese Library

· ·

Accession No. 2251   Index No. 149 - f h

Title   詩 畤 Shih Chi

Classification 万

Subject

References

Author 清閩劉奎等著 Ch'ing, Min Liu Chuan. a others

Edition 家藏版 Private - printed ed. only

Index

Bound in 附外編二卷 謎拾二卷 五冊

Remarks 光緒十九年刻 Block engraving in the 19 year of Kuang Hsü
毛边紙 Mao Pien paper

Accession No. 2252   Index No. 040-cdli

Title 安吳四種 An Wu Szu Chung

Classification 万

Subject

References

Author 清包世臣著 Ch'ing, Pao Shih Shen.

Edition 重校本 ~~orid~~ originally collated edition

Index

Bound in 三十六卷 十六冊 36 Chuan 16 Tsè

Remarks 光緒十四年印 Printed in the 14 year of Kuang Hsü
毛边紙 Mao pien paper

443

The University of Toronto Chinese Library

. . . .

Accession No. 2253   Index No. 053-*lgmg*

Title 廣理學備考 *Kuang Li Hsüeh Pei K'ao*

Classification c-308

Subject

References

Author 清 范部鼎編 *edited by* *Ching, Fan Hao-Ting*

Edition 玉經堂藏版 *Block Preserved in* *Wu-Ching-Tang private printed*

Index

Bound in 1 t'ao 6 ts'ê

Remarks

85

Accession No. 2255   Index No. 030-dzed

Title 呂氏春秋 *Lü Shih Chun Chiu*

Classification

Subject

References

Author 秦相 呂不韋賓客所著   宋陸游評 明凌稚隆批
Chin, Chin Hsi The guests of Lü Pu-Wei (the premier of Chin); Sung, Lu Yu (annotated)
Edition No indication   Ming, Ling Chih-Lung (comment)

Index

Bound in 1 t'áo   8 ts'è

Remarks

445

The University of Toronto Chinese Library

· ·

Accession No. 2256   Index No. 085-<u>Lee</u>gh

Title 清秘述聞 *Ching Pi Shu Wên*

Classification B-   .7

Subject

References

Author 清 法式善編_{edited by} *Ching, Fa Shih-Shan*

Edition 清乾隆辛丑年編 edited in the *Ching, Chien-Lung "Hsien Chou"*
        嘉慶己未王蘇序 *Wang Su's wrote the Introduction in Chia-Ching "Chi-Wei"*

Index Dated — *Ching, Chien-Lung "Hsin-Chou"* 44/1799
                                                46/1781

Bound in 1 tao, 2 ts'è (上,下)

Remarks

The University of Toronto Chinese Library

. . . .

Accession No. 2257   Index No. 149-9929

Title 說文引經攷證 Shuo Wên Yin Ching K'ao Chêng

Classification A — 156 小學 — 訓詁

Subject analogic dictionaries

References

Author 清陳瑑璞等 Ching, Chên Chuan-Hsüeh

Edition 三鳴盦廬刊, 光緒年刊, 連史紙
        San-I-Lu edition, dated Kuang-Hsü period (1875-1908)

Index none

Bound in 1 t'ao, 7 chüan, 附異說 1 chüan, 4 t'sê
Remarks   attached with "I Shuo" 1 chüan

Accession No. 2258   Index No. 187-i22h

Title 騙術奇談 Pien Shu Chi Tán

Classification C—308 雜書一雜文

Subject Miscellaneous writings about all the cheating
stories; with picture.

References

Author 清. 雷君曜編輯 edited by Ching, Lei Chün-Yao

Edition 掃葉山房石印, 連史紙
       Tsao Sao-Yeh-Shan-Fang lithographic edition
       "Lien-Shih" paper

Index A general table of contents for 4 chüan

Bound in 1 tao, 4 chüan, 4 tsê

Remarks

Accession No. 2259   Index No. 118·3329

Title 篆文論語 Chuan Wên Lun Yü

Classification A—134 四書—論語

Subject The Analects

References

Author 清, 吳大澂篆書 Ch'ing, Wu Ta-Ch'êng

Edition 振新書社影印, 篤素堂張德淳藏, 竹紙
Chên-Hsin-Shu-Shê photo-lithographic edition, Tu-Su-Táng
Chang Hsiao-Huan edition, Bamboo paper

Index No index

Bound in 1 tho 4 thê

Remarks

Accession No. 2262   Index No. 149. ℓxii

Title 譚苑醍醐 Tan Yüan Ti Hu

Classification C — 308 雜著 — 雜著

Subject Miscellaneous writings ~~and is~~ and exposition

References

Author Written by 明. 楊慎 撰, Ming, Yang Shên

Edition 重刻明嘉靖本, 竹紙
Reprinted Ming, Chia-Ching's copy
Bamboo paper

Index none

Bound in 1 t̲a̲o̲, 8 chüan, 2 册

Remarks

450

The University of Toronto Chinese Library

. . . .

Accession No. 2266   Index No. 167-3202

Title 金陀續編 Chin Tó Hsü Pien

Classification B—147 載記

Subject Record of contemporary independent state

References

Author 清．岳珂訂編 Ching, Yüeh Kó

Edition 浙江書局刊，光緒九年刻，毛四紙
Chê-Chiang Book Company edition, dated Kuang-Hsü 9/1883.
"Mao-Pien" paper

Index a general table of contents for 30 chüan, +
separate table of contents for each chüan

Bound in 1 tào, 30 chüan, 6 tsê

Remarks

451

The University of Toronto Chinese Library

· ·

Accession No. 2267   102   Index No. 030-b z n q   b

Title 古文纂五種 淮南鴻烈解 戰國策 管子 韓非子
春秋公羊穀梁傳
Ku Wên Tsuan Wu Chung; Huai-Nan, Hung Lieh-Chieh, Chan Kuo Tsê, Kuan Tzŭ,
Classification C-328   *Han Fei Tzŭ, Ch'un Ch'iu Kung Yang Ku Liang Chuan*

Subject

References

Author 張榜纂 *Compiled by*
Chang Pang

Edition *No date given*

Index

Bound in *1 t'ao 6 ts'ê*

Remarks

452

The University of Toronto Chinese Library

. . . .
52

Accession No. 2268   Index No. 038-de k h

Title 妙法蓮華經指掌疏」 Miao Fa Lien Hua Ching Chih Chang
                                          Su

Classification c - 513

Subject

References

Author 賢宗後學通理述   明遠較字
       Hsien-Tsung, Hou Hsüeh-Tung 述; Ming-yüan (revised)
Edition 清乾隆十四年　岫雲寺刊
                     Hsiu-Yün-Ssŭ
       Dated — Ching, Chien-Lung "Chi-Ssŭ" 14/1749

Index

Bound in 1 t'ao   12 ts'ê

Remarks

453

The University of Toronto Chinese Library

. . . .

Accession No. 2270   Index No. 001-ab3 个

Title 七 巧 书 谱 . Chi Chiao Shu Pu

Classification C—238 艺术—杂技

Subject Miscellaneous art of "Chi-Chiao"

References

Author 清 厳 竹 舟 1/2 Ching, Yen Chu-Chou

Edition 听月山房 校刊, 光绪 18 年刻, 连史纸
Ting-Yüeh-Shan-Fang edition, dated Kuang-Hsü 18/1892
"Lien-Shih" paper

Index a general table of contents for 2 Chüan

Bound in 1 t'ao, 2 tsè, 2 Chüan

Remarks

The University of Toronto Chinese Library

. . . .

Accession No. 2272   Index No. 118-i388

Title 纂文老子 Chuan Wên Lao Tzŭ

Classification c-731 道家 Tao Chia (Taoism)

Subject Taoism — "Lao-Tṣe

References

Author 田伏侯秀 Tien Fu-Hou

Edition 家藏版, 单宣纸

Private & family edition, "Tan Hsüan" paper

Index none

Bound in 1 tạo, 1 Tsè

Remarks

The University of Toronto Chinese Library

· ·

Accession No. 2273   Index No. 073-3382

Title (古)目问答 Shu Mu Wên Ta
书

Classification B—342 目錄 — 理論

Subject a general Catalogues of books + writings

References

Author 清, 張之洞 撰, Written by ching. Chang Chih-Tung

Edition 清宣寶刻本, 錦連紙
chu-chia Manuscript and "Mien-Lien" paper, block-printing edition,

Index a general table of contents for a the

Bound in 1 No, a The

Remarks

The University of Toronto Chinese Library

. . . .

102

Accession No. 2274   Index No. 030-ghgb

Title 唐陸宣公集 *Táng Lu Hsüan Kung Chi*

Classification D-43

Subject

References

Author 清, 介春耆英重訂 唐陸贄作品
Ching, Chieh Chun Chi-Ying; Táng, Lu Chih

Edition 道光"丁未"年重刊   京都隆福寺同立堂藏板
Block Preserved in Ching-Tu, Lung-Fu-Ssu, Táng-Li-Táng
Dated — *Tao-kuang "Ting-Wei" 27/1847* ~~privately printed~~

Index

Bound in 1 t'ao   8 ts'e

Remarks

The University of Toronto Chinese Library

....

✓ Accession No. 2275   Index No 073-3cmg

Title 日知薈說 Jih Chih Wei Shuo

Classification C-318 雜家——雜文
                    Tsa Chia — Tsa Wên (Miscellaneous Writing)

Subject Miscellaneous writings

References

                                made by
Author 清, 乾隆帝御製 ∧ Ching, Chien-Lung Emperor

Edition 殿版 palace edition

Index ∧ table of contents only mention how no. of
writings in each chuan.

Bound in / 1套 / 4 chuan, 4 pên

Remarks

The University of Toronto Chinese Library

....

Accession No. 2278   Index No. 085-13/i

Title 潘刻五種 P'an K'ŏ Wu Chung

Classification c-338

Subject

References

Author 吳縣潘氏劚校刊　恩壽重刻
Collated ed. by Wu-Hsien P'an Shih (revised); An Tao (reprinted)
Edition 清光緒年　京都翰文齋藏板
Ching-Tu, Han-Wên-Chai private-printed
Dated — Ching, Kwang-Hsü period 1825—1908

Index

Bound in 1 t'ao　6 ts'ê

Remarks

460

The University of Toronto Chinese Library
· ·

Accession No. ~~7563~~ 2279   Index No. 044-2ih

Title 居業錄 chü yeh Lu

Classification 乙 — 731 區志

Subject ~~a general~~ Taoism

References

Author 明, 胡居仁 著, ~~edited & collated by~~ 張有譽 海枝
Ming, Hu Chü-jên, ~~edited & collated by~~ Chang Yu Yü ~~revised~~

Edition 居補堂校明刻本, 乾隆年刻, 竹紙
Ssŭ-Pu-Tsang edition, dated; Chien-Lung period (1736-1795)
Bamboo paper

Index None

Bound in / t'ao, 8 chüan, 4 tsê

Remarks

461

The University of Toronto Chinese Library

．．．．．．．．．．．．．．．．．．．．．．

Accession No. 2280   Index No. 062-269

Title 戰國策 附札記   Chan Kuo Tsê
                                    Fu Tsa Chi

Classification B-52

Subject

References

Author 漢 高誘注   Annotated by
                  Han, Kao Yu

Edition 湖北崇文書局重刊本   Hu-Pei, Chúng-Wên book company
                                              re-published

        同治己巳年刻   毛邊紙

Index   Dated — Tung-Chih "Chi-Ssǔ" 8/1869
                          "Mao Pien" paper

Bound in 1 t'ao   33 chuan   4 ts'ǔ

Remarks

462

The University of Toronto Chinese Library

. . . .

Accession No. 2281   Index No. 076-みヒみた

Title 欽定清漢對音字式

Classification A - 166 小學 — 韻書

Subject A phonetic dictionary of "Man Wên" and "Han Wên"

References

~~Author~~

Edition
   官版   錦連紙
   Official edition, "Mien-lien" paper

Index
   none

Bound in
   1 tsê , 1 chüan , 1 tao
Remarks

The University of Toronto Chinese Library
. . . .

Accession No. 2282   Index No. 072-2ddg

Title 春林世族譜 Chún Chin Shih Tsu Pu

Classification B —117, — 傳記 — 綜錄
                     Chuan Chi — Tsung Lu (collected biographies)

Subject collected biographies 春林世族
                               "Chun Chin Shih Tsu"

References

Author 清 陳樹峯撰 Written by Ching. Chén Shu-Fêng

Edition 維揚寶翰樓藏板. (道光(康3年刊), 竹紙
        Wei-Yang Pao-Han-Lou edition. Dated Tao-Kuang period (1821-1850)
        Bamboo paper

Index none

Bound in 1 函, 2 冊

Remarks

464

Accession No. 2283   Index No. 030-gzbz

Title 唐開元小說六種 Táng Kái Yüan Hsiao Shuo Liu Chung

Classification 已—368 小說類

Subject novels.

References

Author 清葉德輝輯 compiled by Ching. Yeh Tê-Hui

Edition 葉氏觀古堂刊本, 宣統三年刊, 綿連紙
Yeh-Shih, Kuang-Ku-Táng printed edition, dated Hsüan-Túng 3/1911
"Mien-Lien" paper

Index a general table of contents for 2 tse

Bound in 1 t'ao, 2 tse

Remarks

The University of Toronto Chinese Library

....

12

Accession No. 2285.   Index No. 120-9cim

Title 經字辨體 Ching Tzŭ Pien Ti

Classification A-161

Subject

References

Author 清 邱家煒學 Ch'ing, Ch'iu Chia Wei Hsüeh

Edition 京都二酉齋刊版 Ching-Tu, Ênh-Yu-Chai ~~printe~~ printed
光緒辛巳年重刊. 綿連紙
Doted — Reprinted ed. in
      ^ Kuang-Hsü "Hsin-Ssŭ" 7/1881
Index   "Mien Lien" paper

Bound in 1 t'ao   8 chuan   4 ts'ê

Remarks

466

The University of Toronto Chinese Library

. . . .

Accession No. 2287   Index No. 168-3223

Title 長春真人西記(附 Cháng Chūn Chên Jên Hsi Yu Chi

Classification C — 368 小説家

Subject a narration

References

Author 李志常(撰 *Gwen in oral by*
                        Li Chih-Cháng

Edition 古藉辨囊本集三 竹紙
        Tao & Tsáng chi Yao Pên Wei chi San, Bamboo paper

Index none

Bound in / táo, 2 tsê

Remarks

467

The University of Toronto Chinese Library

· · · · · · · · · · · · · · · · · · ·

Accession No. 2289   Index No. 007-b g j i

Title 五經類編 Wu Ching Lei Pien

Classification C

Subject

References

Author 清周世樟編輯 *edited & compiled by* Ch'ing, Chou Shih Chang

Edition 聚錦堂藏版 Chü Chin Tang
Blocks preserved in

Index

Bound in 二十八卷 十六冊 28 Chuan 16 Tsê

Remarks 乾隆丁未年刻 Block engraving in Ch'ien-Lung "Ting Wei"
竹紙. Bamboo paper

468

The University of Toronto Chinese Library

· ·

Accession No. 2290 ⁹³   Index No. 184-bgdd

Title 飣餖吟集唐 Ting Tou Yin Chi Tang

Classification D-38

Subject

References

Author 清 石贊清集唐詩 黃丙森註釋 Commentaries + annotated by
Ching, Shih Tsan-Ching collected Tang Poems, & Huang Ping-Sên (commentary)

Edition 咸豐年年刊
Dated — Hsien-Fêng "Wu-Wu" 8/1858

Index

Bound in 1 t'ao   4 ts'e

Remarks

The University of Toronto Chinese Library

. . . .

Accession No. 2291   Index No. 057-ㄥ3P3

Title 張氏叢書 Chang Shih Tsung Shu

Classification C-338

Subject

References

Author 清   張澍輯 Compiled by Chu
                    Ching, Chang Shu

Edition 道光元年刊   二酉堂藏板
              辛巳
        Block Preserved in Êrh-Yu-Táng private printed
Dated — Tao-Kuang "Hsin-Ssŭ" 1/1821

Index

Bound in 1 táo 12 tsê

Remarks

470

Accession No. 2292   Index No. 212-zegb

Title 龍泉師友遺稿合編 Lung Chüan Shih Yu I Kao Hê Pien

Classification 万

Subject

References

Compiled by Ch'ing, Li Chiang, Wang Chin Chih

Author 清 李江 王晉之分輯

Edition 家藏版 Private-printed Family ed.

Index

Bound in 八種計十二卷 十二種計十三卷 共六冊

Remarks 光緒年刻 blocks-engraving in Kuang Hsü Period.
竹紙 Bamboo paper

471

Accession No. 2293　　　　　Index No. 030-gd zz

Title 唐宋八大家類選 Tang Sung Pa Ta Chia Lei Hsuan

Classification 8

Subject

References

Author 清儲欣評 ~~Annotated~~ Commentaries by Ching, Ch'u Hsin.

Edition 湖北官書處刊
Block engraving by Hu Pei, official printing office.

Index

Bound in 十四卷六冊　14 Chuan 6 Tsé

Remarks 光緒年刻 Block-engraving in Kuang Hsü period.
竹紙 Bamboo paper

The University of Toronto Chinese Library

. . . .

Accession No. 2294   Index No. 106-dLg3

Title 皇清經解敬修堂編目 *Huang Ching Ching Chieh Ching Hsiu Tang Pien Mu*

Classification β-337

Subject

References

Author 清 陶治元等編輯 *edited & compiled by Ching, Tao Shih-Yüan and others*

Edition 學海堂原版 *Hsüeh-Hai-Tang's original copy*

光緒丙戌年
Dated — Kuang-Hsü "Ping-Hsü" 12/1886

Index

Bound in 1 t'ao   16 chuan   4 ts'ê

Remarks

The University of Toronto Chinese Library

. . . .

58

Accession No. 2295   Index No. 151-zhdg

Title 豆棚閒話 Tou Pêng Hsien Hua

Classification C-387

Subject

References

Author 艾衲衲居士原本　百懶道人重訂
Ai-Na-Chu-Shih's original copy; Pai-Lai-Tao-Jen (revised)

Edition 嘉慶乙丑年鐫　致和堂梓行
　　　　　　　　　　Chih-Ho-Táng
Dated — Chia-Ching "I-Chóu" 10/1805

Index

Bound in 1 táo   4 tsê

Remarks

474

The University of Toronto Chinese Library

· ·

Accession No. 2296   Index No. 031-bzmg

Title 四聲釋義 Ssŭ Yin Shih I

Classification A — 151 小學

Subject

A dictionary with explanation of the four ~~tones~~
tones

References

Author 清, 鄭長庚 輯 *Compiled by*
^Ching. Chêng Cháng-Kêng

Edition 東鹿堂藏板, 道光十一年刻, 竹紙.

Block preserved ^in Tung-Lu-Táng edition, ^*Dated* Tao-Kuang 11/1831
            Bamboo paper

Index
    none

Bound in / t'ào, 12 chüan, 12 ts'ê

Remarks

The University of Toronto Chinese Library
. . . .

Accession No. 2297   16.   Index No. 037- hdi

Title 大清光緒新法令 Ta Ching Kuang Hsü Hsin Fa Ling

Classification B-302

Subject

References

Author 商務印書館編譯所編輯   edited & Compiled by   Shang Wu-Yin-Shu-Kuan Pien I So

Edition 清宣統元年八月再版
上海商務印書館發行
     Shanghai, Shang-Wu book company published

Index   Dated — Ching, Hsüen-Tung "Chi-Yu" 1/1909 Aug.
     second ed.

Bound in 4 tao, 20 ts'ê

Remarks

The University of Toronto Chinese Library

. . . .

5

Accession No. 2299   Index No. 053-と孔と3

Title 康熙字典 Káng Hsi Tzŭ Tien

Classification A-161

Subject

References

Author 清 張玉書等奉勅纂 Compiled & by order
^ Ching, Chang Yü-shu and others

Edition 三胡北崇文書局重刊 Hu-Pei, Chung Wên book company second ed

光緒元年刊 綿連紙
乙亥   "Mien Lien" paper

Index Dated — Kuang-Hsü "I-Hai" 1/1875

Bound in 6 t'ao 40 ts'ê   .

Remarks

Accession No. 2300   Index No. 042-3mdg

Title 小學集解 (朱子小學集解) Hsiao Hsüeh Chi Chieh
                                        (Chu Tzŭ Hsiao Hsüeh Chi Chieh)

Classification C-13

Subject

References

Author 清 張伯行纂輯 (康熙五十年). *Compiled by* Ching, Chang Po-Hang

Edition 道光三十年重刊 *Second ed.*
        庚戌
Dated — Tao-Kuang "Kěng-Hsü" 30/1850

Index

Bound in 1 táo 4 tsʻú

Remarks

The University of Toronto Chinese Library

. . . .

15

Accession No. 2301   Index No. 106-dhed

Title 皇朝詞林典故 Huang Chao Tzü Lin Tien Ku

Classification B-257 (?)

Subject

References

Author 清 張廷玉等修輯 Edited & Compiled by Ching, Chang Ting-Yü and others

Edition 光緒十三年重鐫 Dated — Kuang-Hsü "Ting-Hai" 13/1887

Index

Bound in 4 tao, 34 ts'é

Remarks

The University of Toronto Chinese Library

....

Accession No. 2302   Index No. 085- e d k c

Title 況阮盦記五種 Huang Yüan An Chi Wu Chung

Classification C

Subject

References 頤

Author 況周儀記 take notes by Huang Chou I

Edition 家藏版 Private- printed edition

Index

Bound in 共 八卷 四冊 8 Chüan 4 Tsê

Remarks 毛边紙 Mao-Pien paper

藍字 Printed in blue

480

The University of Toronto Chinese Library

. . . .

Accession No. 2303   Index No. 167-jɪɡᵉ

Title
鎮撫事宜四卷 附 西藏圖說一卷
Chên Fu Shih I Ssŭ Chüan, Fu Hsi Tsang Tû Shuo I Chüan

Classification
B-197 地理一書屬

Subject

References

Author
清, 松筠 Ching, Sung Chün Yün

Edition
道光三年夏, 寫刻版
dated Tao-Kuang 3 summer/1823. manuscript

Index
none

Bound in
1 tâo, 4 chüan, 2 tsê

Remarks   Hsi-Tsang-Tû-Shuo 1 chüan is attached

Place, publisher, date —

481

The University of Toronto Chinese Library

. . . .

Accession No. 2315   Index No. 189-397ᵇ

Title 高厚蒙求 *Kao Hou Mêng Chiu*

Classification ~~B~~ C 138

Subject *astronomy and Geography*

References

Author 清，徐朝俊纂 *Ching, Hsü Chao-Chün* Compiled by

Edition 同文館聚珍版，光緒十三年刊，綿連紙 *Tung-Wên-Kuan movable-type edition, dated Kuang-Hsü 13/1887, "Mien-Lien" paper*

Index *separate table of content for each tsʻe*

Bound in *1 tʻào, 4 tsʻê*

Remarks

88

Accession No. 2306   Index No. 113-l3eg

Title 禪門佛事全部 Ch'an Mên Fo Shih Chüan Pu

Classification C-513

Subject

References

Author 玉樂山等較刊重印募資刻印 ~~engraved-Print~~ by Yü Lo-Shan and others

Edition 光緒壬午年重刊   京都前門外楊梅竹斜街永盛齋
        Dated—Kuang-Hsü "Jên-Wu"   刻字鋪存板
             8/1882
                    Ching-Tu, Ch'ien-Mên Wai, Yang Mei-Chu-
                    Hsieh-Chieh, Yung Shêng Chai, Kó Tzŭ
Index   Pu

Bound in 1 t'ao   1 ts'ê

Remarks

The University of Toronto Chinese Library

. . . .

Accession No. 2307   Index No. 167-3293

Title   金剛經贅解   Chin Kang Ching Pang Chieh

Classification   C513 釋家 Shih Chia

Subject

References

Author   湯輦召   Táng Nien-Chao.

Edition   石印本 Lithographic edition
          民國八年印 dated Republic 8/1919

Index   油光紙 "Yu-Kuang" paper

Bound in   1 tào ttáu

Remarks

The University of Toronto Chinese Library

• •

Accession No. 2308   Index No. 149-989i

Title 說文發疑 *Shuo Wên Fa I*

Classification A 161- 小學 ~~訓詁~~ 字書

Subject

References

Author 張行孚
清 ~~俞樾~~ *Ching, Yü Yüeh Chang Hsing-Fu*

Edition

光緒九年刻 *dated Kuang-Hsü 9/1883*

Index

A general table of contents for 6 chüan

Bound in

1 t'ao, 2 ts'ê, 6 chüan

Remarks

Accession No. 2309   Index No. 140-1362

Title 董解元絃索西廂記 Tung Chieh Yüan Hsüan So Hsi Hsiang Chi

Classification C 368 小說家

Subject

References

Author 顧渚山樵點定 Punctuated by Ku Chu-Shan-Chiao

Edition 夢鳳樓暖紅室刊 block-engraving by Mêng-Fêng-Lou Nuan-Hung-Shih

綿連紙 "Mien-Lien" paper

Index

Bound in 1 táo 4 chuan 2 tsê

Remarks

The University of Toronto Chinese Library
. . . .

Accession No. 2312   Index No. 074-bdch

Title 有唐明賢逸翰 Yu Ming Ming Hsien I Han

Classification D—73 總集一文

Subject a general collection of prose

References

Author 清, 謝世伯輯 雲/ Compiled & engraved by   Ching, Hsieh Shih-Po

Edition 漢皋文淵堂向藏板, 咸豐之年刊, 綿連紙
Han Kao. Wên-Yüan Book company, edition dated Hsien-Fêng 1/1851
"Mien-Lien" paper

Index a general table of contents for 2 Chüan

Bound in 1 t'ao, 2 Chüan, 4 ts'e

Remarks

The University of Toronto Chinese Library

· ·

61

Accession No. 2313   Index No. 085-9hh3

Title 洗冤錄詳義 Hsi Yüan Lu Hsiang I

Classification C-43

Subject

References

Author 宋 宋慈著 Sung, Sung Tzŭ

Edition 清光緒癸未秋貴州臬署重刊

            Kui-Chou, Hsien-Shu (local government reprinted)

Index Dated — Ching, Kuang-Hsü "Kuei-Wei" 9/1883

Bound in 1 t'áo 2 ts'è¹

Remarks

The University of Toronto Chinese Library

. . . .

Accession No.2314   Index No. 046-e d d z

Title 岳忠武王文 Yüeh Chung Wu Wang Wên

Classification g

Subject

References

Author 宋岳飛撰, 清黄邦寧纂修 — Written by Sung Yüeh Fei.
Compiled & edited by Ching.
Edition 清郝迂年補修版 — Huang Pang Nin.
Amended ed. by Cheng, Hao Yen Nien.

Index

Bound in 四卷四册 4 Chuan 4 Tsé

Remarks 嘉慶二十一年刊 Engraving in 21 of Chia-ching.
土綿連紙 Cotton paper sized with alum

489

The University of Toronto Chinese Library

. . . .

Accession No. 2315   Index No. 031-bgic

Title 四裔編年表 Ssŭ I Pien Nien Piao

Classification B.—22 編年

Subject Annals

References

Author 美國，林樂知，中國，嚴良勳同譯，清李鳳苞
_{^Collected + edited by}
Lin Lo-Chih (American) and Yen Liang-Hsün translated; Chǐng, Li
Edition 原刻本，綿連紙。   Fêng-Pao edited (彙編)
_{^engraving}
original ^copy, "Mien-Lien" paper

Index none

Bound in 1 t'ao, 4 ts'ê

Remarks

Accession No. 2316   Index No. 040-293b

Title 宗室王公世職章京爵秩襲次全表
Tsung Shih Wang Kung Shih Chih Chang Ching Chüeh Chih Hsi Tʻzŭ Chüan Piao

Classification β-157

Subject

References

Author 清候選知府牟其汶編纂 Edited & Compiled by
Ching, Mou Chi-Wên

Edition 清宗人府奉欽旨刊印 Block-Print by
Ching, Tsung Jen-Fu
光緒三十二年十二月
Dated — Kuang-Hsü "Ping-Wu" 32/1906 December.

Index

Bound in 1 tao, 10 tsʻê

Remarks

491

The University of Toronto Chinese Library

. . . .

Accession No. 2317   Index No. 162-gونc

Title 通鑑學要 *Tùng Chien Lan Yao*

Classification C-348

Subject

References

Author 清 姚培謙 張景星 同錄 *Copied by Ching, Yao Pei-Chien and Chang Ching-Hsing*

Edition 乾隆辛巳年鎬 飛鴻堂藏板 *Work preserved in Fei-Hung-Tang private printed*

Dated — *Chien-Lung "Hsin-Ssŭ" 26/1761*

Index

Bound in 1 t'ao 20 ts'ê

Remarks

The University of Toronto Chinese Library

. . . .

Accession No. 2319   Index No. - 077-1 c 39

Title 歷代石經考 Li Tai Shih Ching Kǎo

Classification A-137

Subject

References

Author 張國淦著 Chang Kuo-Kan

Edition 燕京大學國學研究所印 Yenching University, Kuo-Hsüeh Yen (Chinese literature studies)
民國十九年十二月 Chiu Sou published printed
Dated — Ming-Kuo 19/1930 Dec.

Index

Bound in 1 tao, 3 ts'ê

Remarks

The University of Toronto Chinese Library

· ·

Accession No. 2320   Index No. 061-78c

Title 息縣志 Hsi Hsien Chih

Classification B-194

Subject Gazeteer of Hsi Hsien, Honan

References

Author 清 劉光輝等重修 *Revised ed by* Ching, Liu Kuang-Hui and others

Edition 官版 嘉慶廿四年刊 *Official ed.*
Dated — Chia-Ching "

Index

Bound in 1 t'ao 8 Chuan

Remarks This a the edition as the etiat of Accession No. 2656.
The printing is much clearer.

494

The University of Toronto Chinese Library

. . . .

Accession No. 2321   Index No. 030-他 ﾁ c

Title 商城縣志 Shang Chêng Hsien Chih

Classification B-194

Subject Gazeteer of Shang-ch'êng Hsien

References

Author 清 武開吉等重修 Revised ed. by
                          Ching, Wu Kai Chi and others

Edition 官板 嘉慶八年刊 Official ed.
Dated — Chia-Ching "Kuei-Hai" 8/1803

Index

Bound in 2 t'ao   14 Chuan   12 ts'ê

Remarks

The University of Toronto Chinese Library

. . . .

Accession No. 2323   Index No. 042-zize

Title 小題文府 Hsiao Ti Wên Fu

Classification D-53 總集

Subject

References

Author 無

Edition 上海點石齋縮印 Shanghai, Tien-shih-chai printed
         袖珍本   pocket edition
         光緒十七年印   dated Kuang-Hsü 17, 1891
Index   綿連紙 木刻板 "Mien-Lien" paper, wood block

Bound in 1 Hao 20 Ts'i

Remarks

The University of Toronto Chinese Library

. . . .

Accession No. 2324   126   Index No. 102-293h

Title 留餘草堂叢書 Liu Yü Tsao Táng Tsúng Shu

Classification c-33ρ

Subject

References

Author 清 展 劉承幹校   Collated by   Ching. Liu Chêng-Kan

Edition 留餘草堂刊   Block-engraving in   Liu-Yü-Tsou Tsáo-Táng published

Index

Bound in 1 táo   12 tsè

Remarks

The University of Toronto Chinese Library

....

Accession No. 2325 [128]   Index No. 030-大㐖㐖P

Title 嘉業堂叢書 *Chia Yeh Táng Tsúng Shu*

Classification c-338

Subject

References

Author 諸家著 *Some Famous Writers*

Edition 清 劉氏嘉業堂刊
Block-engraving in Ching, Liu-Shih, Chia-Yeh-Táng published

Index

Bound in 1 *t'ào* 8 *ts'ê*

Remarks

The University of Toronto Chinese Library

. . . .

98

Accession No. 2326   Index No. 037-g h di

Title 大清光緒時憲書 Ta Ching Kuang Hsu Shih Hsien Shu

Classification β-157

Subject

References

Author 清 欽天監編 edited by Ching, Chin Tien-chien

Edition 官版   白紙   official ed.
          white paper

Index

Bound in 1 t'ao   7 ts'ê

Remarks

The University of Toronto Chinese Library

. . . .

Accession No. 2327   Index No. 037-3 h d i

Title 大清光緒年時憲書 Ta Ching Kuang Hsü Nien Shih Hsien Shu

Classification B-157

Subject

References

Author edited by Ching, Chin T'ien-Chien.

Edition

Index

Bound in 2 t'ao   15 ts'ê

Remarks

The University of Toronto Chinese Library
. . . .

Accession No. 2328 ¹⁸   Index No. 037-ᵹ ʰ c ₑ

Title 大清同治年時憲書 Ta ch'ing T'ung Chih Nien Shih Hsien Shu

Classification β-157

Subject

References

Author 清 欽天監編 *edited by* ^ ch'ing, Chin Tien-Chien

Edition 官版 粉紙 *official ed.*
      "fêng" paper

Index

Bound in 1 t'ao 9 ts'è

Remarks

The University of Toronto Chinese Library

. . . .

                              18
Accession No. 2329   Index No. 037-习之习之

Title 大清咸豐年時憲書 Ta Ching Hsien Fêng Nien Shih Hsien Shu

Classification B-157

Subject

References

Author 清 欽天監編 Ching, Chin Tien-Chien

Edition 官版 粉紙 official ed.
          "fêng" paper

Index

Bound in 1 t'ao   5 ts'e

Remarks

The University of Toronto Chinese Library

. . . .

Accession No. 2330   Index No. 095-y l c j

Title 立機直講 Hsüan Chi Chih Chiang

Classification C 368

Subject

References

Author 楊學淵輯 *Compiled by* Yang Hsüeh Yüan

Edition 長沙積善小補堂校刊
collated ed. in Chang Sha, Chi Shan ~~ch~~ Hsiao Pu Táng

Index

Bound in 三卷一冊 3 Chuan 1 Tsê

Remarks 民國辛酉年刊
Block engraving in the year of "Hsien-yu" of
                                    the Republic

The University of Toronto Chinese Library

．．．．．．．．．．．．．．．．．．．．．．．．．．

Accession No. 2331   Index No. 037-8rgc

Title 大觀亭志 Ta Kuan Ting Chih

Classification B 194

Subject

References

Author 清李丙榮編輯 *edited & compiled by* Ch'ing, Li Ping gung

Edition 丹徒李氏印於皖城衛齋
Printed by Tan Tu Li Shih in Huan City (Anhwei) Wei Chai.

Index

Bound in 上下二卷, 一冊 2 chüan, 1 Tsé

Remarks 宣統辛亥年印 Printing in Hsüan Tung "Hsin-Hai"
洋紙 imported Paper

504

The University of Toronto Chinese Library

. . . .

Accession No. 2332   Index No. 120-cjdz

Title 紀慎先生求雨全書 Chi Shen Hsien Sheng Chiu Yü Chuan Shu

Classification C308

Subject

References

Author 清 紀大奎 著 Ch'ing, Chi Ta Kuei

Edition 刻鵠齋版

Block-printing'e Ku Chai Block-printing edition

Index

Bound in 上下兩卷一冊 2 chüan 1 Tsê

Remarks 光緒年刻連史紙 Engraved in the year of "Kuanghsü" 無套. Lien shih paper.

The University of Toronto Chinese Library

. . . .

Accession No. 2333   Index No. 061-imid

Title 感應編印譜 Kan Yin Pien Yin Pu

Classification C 308

Subject

References

Author 清 汪學成 撰 Written by Ch'ing, Wang Hsueh Cheng

Edition 家藏版 Private-printed edition

Index

Bound in 一冊 1 Tsé

Remarks 綿連紙 Mien Lien paper

506

Accession No. 2334   Index No. 007-ʒleo

Title 二樹紫籐花館印選 Er Shu Tzŭ Tĕng Hua Kuan Yin Hüan

Classification C 233

Subject

References

Author 清周彦戚選 Selected by Chʻing, Chou Yen Wei

Edition 砵墨套印 Printed in red and black

Index

Bound in 一冊 1 Tsé

Remarks 綿連紙 Mien-Lien paper

The University of Toronto Chinese Library

· ·

Accession No. 2335   Index No. 085-gghg

Title 海島算經 Hai Tao Suan Ching

Classification C 138
~~B 57~~

Subject

References

Author 晉劉徽撰 Written by ∧Chin, Liu Hui

Edition 武英殿聚珍版
Wu Ying Tien movable-type edition

Index

Bound in 一全回 1 Tsk

Remarks 乾隆年版 Dated-Chien-Lung period
竹紙 Bamboo paper

The University of Toronto Chinese Library

. . . .

Accession No. *2336*   Index No. *030-hz*

<u>Title</u> 荀子 Shang Tzu

<u>Classification</u> *C43*

<u>Subject</u>

<u>References</u>

Commentaries & annotations by

<u>Author</u> 明，楊慎，顧郡初許釋 *Ming, Yang Shen, &*
                                              Ku Lin Ch'u
<u>Edition</u> 朝爽閣版

Chao Shuang Ko Black-printing edition

<u>Index</u>

<u>Bound in</u> 一册 *1 Tsê*

<u>Remarks</u> 竹紙 *bamboo paper*

509

The University of Toronto Chinese Library

. . . .

Accession No. *2337*   Index No. *066-giq*

Title 教諭語 *Chiao Yü Yü*

Classification *C 731*

Subject

References

Author 清謝金鑾撰, *Written by* *Ch'ing Hsieh Chin Luan*

Edition 福建省城吳玉．田刻坊 *Publisher-Fukien Wu Yü T'ien* 藏版 *Block-preserved.*

Index

Bound in 一冊 *I Ts'e*

Remarks 綿連紙 *Mien Lien paper*

The University of Toronto Chinese Library

· ·

Accession No. 2328   Index No. 113-ldpc

Title 禪林寶訓筆說 Shan Lin Pao Hsün Pi Shui

Classification C 513

Subject

References

Author 釋智祥註 Annotated by Shih Chih Hsiang

Edition

Index

Bound in 二卷一冊 2 Chüan 1 Tsé

Remarks 乾隆年刻 Block-printed in Chien Lung
竹紙 Bamboo paper

511

Accession No. 2339   Index No. 061-cmi

Title 志學編 Chih Hsueh Pien

Classification C 308

Subject

References

Author 清余寅止編次 edited in order by Ch'ing, Yu Yin Chih

Edition 務本堂 藏版 Block preserved in Wu Pen T'ang

Index

Bound in 上下二卷一冊 2 Chüan 1 Tsé

Remarks 光緒元年重刊 Reprinted in the first year of "Kuang Hsü"
毛边紙 "Mao-Pien" paper

The University of Toronto Chinese Library

....

Accession No. 2340   Index No. 124-eecl

Title 翊翊齋遺書 I I Chai I Shu

Classification 方 33

Subject

References

Author 清馬嗣飛撰, Ching, Ma Kê Fei Written by

Edition 家藏版 Private-painted edition family

Index

Bound in 四卷一冊 4 Chuan 1 Tsé

Remarks 計二種
毛边纸 Mao. Pien Paper

Accession No. 2341   Index No. 149-h9cd

Title 論語要略 Lung Yu Yao Liao

Classification A 134

Subject

References

Author 清許珏輯 Compiled by Ching, Hsü Chüeh

Edition 無錫許氏刊 Block-engraved by Wu Hsi, Hsü Shih

Index

Bound in 1 Tsè

Remarks 連史紙 "Lien Shih" paper

The University of Toronto Chinese Library

. . . .

Accession No. 2342   Index No. 085 — j b z d

Title 滄來自記年譜 Tsang Lai Tzu Chi Nien Pu

Classification B 117

Subject

References

Author 清滄來 撰 Written by Ching Yü Tsang Lai.

Edition 四庫全書館纂 Compiled by Szu K'u Chuan Shu School.
~~四庫全書~~, 家藏版 Private family edition.

Index

Bound in   1 Tsé

Remarks 白紙寫刻本 White paper printed from copied ed.

515

Accession No. 2343 · Index No. 037-zmba

Title 大學古本質言 Ta Hsueh Ku Pen Chih Yen

Classification C

Subject

References

Author 清劉沅著 Ching, Liu Yüan

Edition 竹陰書屋重鐫本

Index

Bound in 一冊 1 Ts'e

Remarks 光緒庚辰年刻 block engraving in Kuang-Hsü "Keng
白紙 White paper

Accession No. 2344   Index No. 061-e i i e

Title 急就篇註 Chi Chiu Pien Chu

Classification C 308

Subject

References

Author 顏敬章編, 姚士彝校. edited by Yen Yü Chang.
Collated by Yao Shih Lin

Edition

Index

Bound in 4 Chüan 1 Tsê

Remarks

Accession No. 2345　　　　Index No. 029-gh

Title　又問　Yu Wen

Classification　C 308

Subject

References

Author　清劉沅著　Ching, Liu Yuan

Edition　樂善堂藏版
Block-Preserved Li Shan Tang

Index

Bound in　一冊　1 Tsê

Remarks　光緒丙戌年重刊 Reprinted edition in Kuang-Hsü
白紙　White Paper　"Ping-Ying"

Accession No. 2346   Index No. 009-gg

Title 俗言 Su Yen

Classification C 308

Subject

References

Author 清彭光譽撰 ∧Written by Ch'ing, P'êng Kuang Yü

Edition 進呈本 Presented to the Throne edition
文光齋刻版
Wen Kuang Chai Block printing edition

Index

Bound in 一冊 1 Tsê

Remarks 綿連紙 Mien-lien paper

The University of Toronto Chinese Library

· ·

Accession No. 2347   Fan   Index No. 169-fð69

Title 閩縣洪球珣巳先生梅譜

Classification   Min Hsien Hung Chiu Chi Hsien Sheng Mei Pú
    B-107

Subject

References

Author 趙爾巽 Written by Chao

Edition 京華印書局永印, 丙寅首夏 The first summer of "Ping yin"
~~Printing Ping~~
Printing in Ching Hua book Co.

Index

Bound in 1 Tsé

Remarks

520

The University of Toronto Chinese Library

．．．．．．．．．．．．．．．．．．．．．．．．．．．．

Accession No. 2348   Index No. 147-mdeg

Title 覺世真經註解 Chiao Shih Chen Ching Chu Chieh

Classification C 512

Subject

References

Author

Edition 樂興善齋鐫本
Le Yü Shan Chai edition

Index

Bound in 一冊 1 Tsé

Remarks 道光癸未年刊 Block-engraving in "Tao-Kuang"
綿連紙 Mien Lien Paper   Wei

The University of Toronto Chinese Library

....

Accession No. 2349   Index No. 039-cizi

Title 存業八編 T'sun Yeh Pa Pien

Classification C33

Subject

References

Author 清原良著 Ch'ing, Yüan Liang

Edition 聽潮居版 Ting chao chu block

Index

Bound in 一冊 1 Tŝè

Remarks 白紙 White-paper

Accession No. 2350   Index No. 037-zhee

Title 大悲神咒 Ta Pei Shen Chou

Classification C 5/3

Subject

References

Author 唐 釋伽梵達磨譯 Translated by T'ang,
Shih Chia Fan Ja Mo

Edition 上海成文厚書局石印本 Shanghai, Cheng Wen
附圖像 Hou Book Company Lithographic edition

Index

Bound in 一冊 1 Tse

Remarks 光緒甲申年印 Printed in Kuang-Hsi "Chai Shin

Accession No. 2351   Index No. 167-m f

Title 鐸書 To Shu

Classification C 338

Subject

References

Author 明 韓霖 撰, Written by Ming. Han Lin

Edition 新會陳氏校刊鉛印

Collated edition by Hsin Hui Chén Shih
Type-setting edition

Index

Bound in 一冊 1 Tsé

Remarks 毛边纸 Mao. Pien Paper

524

The University of Toronto Chinese Library

· ·

Accession No. *2352*　　　　　Index No. *061-ccif*

Title 忍字輯略 *Jên Tzu Chi Lueh*

Classification *C308*

Subject

References

Compiled by Ching, Chu Hsi Chen

Author 清朱錫珍原輯

Edition 慕玄父重刊 *Reprinted edition by Mu Hsüan Fu*

鉛印本 *Type-setting edition*

Index

Bound in 五卷一冊 *5 Chuan 1 Tsê*

Remarks 民國十年印 *Painting in the 10th Year of the Republic*

The University of Toronto Chinese Library

. . . .

Accession No. 2354   Index No. 128-9zih

Title 聖門諸賢輯傳 Sheng Mên Chu Hsien Chi Chuan

Classification B 102

Subject

References

Author 清查光泰輯, *Compiled by* Chiang. Ch'a Kuang Tai

Edition 家藏版 Private-Printed edition.

Index

Bound in 一冊 1 tsê

Remarks 綿連紙 "Mien-Lien" paper

526

Accession No. 2355   Index No. 031-6338

Title 四十二章經講錄 Szu Shih Erh Chang Ching Chiang Lu

Classification A 137

Subject

References

Author 羅庸 Lo Yung.

Edition 民國十六年四月再版
Republished in the 16 year of the Republic.

Index 北京和濟印刷局
Printing in Peiching, Hai chi printing book Co..

Bound in 1 tsé

Remarks

The University of Toronto Chinese Library

· ·

Accession No. 2356   Index No. 036-kc f j

Title 夢仙詩稿 Mêng Hsien Shih Kao

Classification D 38

Subject

References

Author 清 孫雲 著 Ch'ing, Sun Yün

Edition 珂羅版鉛印 K'ê Lo type-setting edition.

Index

Bound in 一冊 1 Tsê

Remarks 連史紙 Lien shih paper

528

· ·

Accession No. 2357   Index No. 037-子ㄌㄓㄉ

Title 大潛山房詩鈔 Ta Chʻien Shan Fang Shih Chʻao

Classification 方33

Subject

References

Author 清劉銘傳著 Chʻing, Liu Ming Chuan.

Edition 中國圖書公司鉛印
Type-setting editon, Chung Kuo Tʻu shu Co.

Index

Bound in 一冊　1 Tʻsʻe

Remarks 油光紙

Accession No. 2358　　　　　Index No. 003-dfg2

Title　主制辟徵　Chu Chih Chüin Cheng

Classification　C971

Subject

References

Author　馮若望撰　Written by Tang Je Wang

Edition　鉛印本　Type-setting edition

Index

Bound in　一函二卷　1 tsé 2 chüan

Remarks　毛邊紙　Mao-Pien paper.

The University of Toronto Chinese Library

. . . .

Accession No. 2360 A - B   Index No. Ⓐ 146-zmce

Title Ⓐ 西藏紀述   Ⓑ 117- nzac
       Hsi Tsang Chi Shu   Ⓑ 章谷屯志略.
Classification   Chang Ku T'un Chih Liao.
                  B-14
Subject   B-194, B 217

References

Author Hsi Tsang Chi Shu was Written by Chang Kai. (張海)

Edition Chang Ku T'un Chih Liao was Compiled & Collected by
                                    Wu Te Hsü & Tzu
        Kuang   Hsi Pu.
        Dated – Hsü period

Index

Bound in 2 chüan, 1 tsê

Remarks

532

Accession No. 2361   Index No. 009-Ji99

Title 人道大義錄 Jen Tao Ta Yi Lu

Classification C 33

Subject

References

Author 清夏震武撰 Written by Cling, Hsia Chen Wu

Edition 活字版 Movable type edition
大字印 Large character printing.

Index

Bound in 一冊 1 Ts'e

Remarks 毛边纸 Mao. Pien Paper

The University of Toronto Chinese Library

．．．．．．．．．．．．．．．．．．．．．．．．．．

Accession No. 2362   Index No. 073-gczk

Title 曼衍心漚 Man Yen Hsin Lou

Classification C 30β

Subject

References

Author 殭蠶子著 Chiang Ts'an Tzu

Edition 家藏版 Private-printed edition

Index

Bound in 三卷一冊 3 Chüan 1 Ts'e

Remarks 連史紙 Lien-Shih paper

534

Accession No. 2363   Index No. 157-jcjl

Title 謇齋賸墨 Chien Chai Sheng Mo

Classification C308

Subject

References

Author 清英華撰 *Written by,* Ching, Ying Hua

Edition 家藏版 Private-printed edition.

Index

Bound in 一冊 1 Title

Remarks 毛边纸 Mao-pien paper

The University of Toronto Chinese Library

. . . .

Accession No. 2364   Index No. 030-bzlc

Title 古文辭約編 Ku Wen Tzŭ Yüeh Pien

Classification D 73

Subject

References

Author 李剛己選 Selected by Li Kang chi.

Edition 柏香書屋校印 Pai Hsiang Shu Wu
銘印大字本 Type-setting ~~edition with~~ with large
Characters ~~edition~~.

Index

Bound in 一册 1 Tsè

Remarks 毛边纸 Mao-pien paper

536

The University of Toronto Chinese Library

. . . .

Accession No. 2365   Index No. 009-ㄡㄎ

Title 人格 Jên Kê

Classification C 33

Subject

References

Author 唐文治著 Tang Wen chih

Edition 鉛印本 Type-setting edition

Index

Bound in 一冊 1 Tsè

Remarks 毛边纸 "mao-pien" paper

The University of Toronto Chinese Library

. . . .

Accession No. 2366   Index No. 146-3g子e

Title 西寧等處軍務紀略

Hsi Nin Têng Chu Chün Wu Chi Lüeh

Classification C33

Subject

References

Author 奎順 K'uei shun.

Edition 光緒年

Dated — Kuang-Hsü period.

Index

Bound in 1Tsè

Remarks

Accession No. 2367   Index No. 075- e h g h

Title 柏堂師友言行記 Pai Tang shih Yu Yen Hsing chi.

Classification c 13

Subject

References

Author 清方宗誠撰 Written by Ching, Fang Chung Cheng

Edition 蓬萊慕玄父校刊本
Collated from block print edition by Pêng Lai Mu Hsüan Fu

Index 鉛印 Type-setting edition

Bound in 四卷一册 4 chüan, 1 Tsê

Remarks 洋白毛边纸 Imported White Mao-pien paper

The University of Toronto Chinese Library

....

Accession No. 2369   Index No. 039-9 3 l e

Title 孫子選註 Sun Tzu Hsüan Chu

Classification C 33

Subject

References

Author 夏壽田奉 命選註 Selected & annotated order by Hsia Shou Tien.

Edition 硃格石印本 lithographic edition in red columns.

Index

Bound in 一冊　1 Tsé

Remarks 綿連紙 Mien-Lien paper

540

. . . .

Accession No. 2370   Index No. 044 - e b z 0

Title 居仁日覽 chü jen jih Lan

Classification B 297

Subject

References

Author 阮忠樞進呈 Presented to the Throne by Yüan chung Shu.

Edition 石印本 Lithographic edition

Index

Bound in 一冊 1 Tse

Remarks 宣紙 a kind of cotton paper made in Hsüin Ch'eng.

541

The University of Toronto Chinese Library

. . . .

Accession No. 2371   Index No. 044-e b go

Title 居仁日覽 Chü gen gih Lan

Classification B 297

Subject

References

Author

Edition 內史鹽館本石印

Index

Bound in 一冊 1 Title

Remarks 民國四年印 Printed in The 4th year of the Republic
錦連紙 Mien-Lien paper

The University of Toronto Chinese Library

· ·

Accession No. 2372   Index No. 101-izdg

Title 篆文孝經 Chuan Wen Hsiao Ching

Classification A-121

Subject

References

Author 吳大澂 Wu Ta chêng.

Edition
光緒乙酉季 Dated- Kuang-Hsü "I-Yu"
上海同文書局石印
Index ~~Printed in~~ Lithographie ed. in Tung Wen Book Co.
                                                    Shanghai.

Bound in 1 Tsé

Remarks

The University of Toronto Chinese Library

．．．．．．．．．．．．．．．．．．．．．．．．．．

Accession No. 2373   Index No. 156-e b j d

Title 越台輿頌 Yüeh T'ai Yü Sung

Classification 63

Subject

References

Author 清崇室督英著 Ch'ing & Tsung Shih Ch'ü Ying.

Edition 寫刻本 ~~Ed~~ Printed from copied ed.
         紅格印 Printed in red columns.

Index

Bound in 一冊 1 Tsé

Remarks 綿連紙 Mien-Lien paper

. . . .

Accession No. 2374   Index No. 032-leic

Title 墨法輯要 Mo Fa Chi Yao

Classification C308

Subject

References

Author 明沈繼孫撰 ，Written by Ming, Shen Chi Sun

Edition 涉園影印文，Photo-lithographic ed. by She Yuan

津閣舊鈔本 Ching Ko old manuscript.

Index

Bound in 一冊 1 Tsé

Remarks 緜連紙 Mien-Lien paper

The University of Toronto Chinese Library
. . . .

Accession No. 2375   Index No. 001-bhcz

Title 三國志小樂府 San Kuo Chih Hsiao Yüeh Fu

Classification C 368

Subject

References

Author 熊寶泰箋 Compiled by Hsiung Pao Tai

Edition 嘉慶戊辰年 dated: Chia-ching "Wu Shen" period

Index

Bound in 1 Tsè

Remarks

Accession No. 2376   Index No. 154-ecje

Title 貴池縣沿革表 Kuei Chih Hsien Yen Kê Piao

Classification B 187

Subject

References

Author 清劉世珩撰 Written by Ch'ing Liu Shih Hang

Edition 聖廟叢書本 Chien Ch'ing separate edition from a Collectanea
竹宋精刊 Fang Sung Fine printed edition.

Index

Bound in 一卷一冊 1 Chüan 1 Tsê

Remarks 日本皮紙

The University of Toronto Chinese Library

· ·

Accession № 2377　　　　　Index № 173-2 b z z

Title 雲臺二十八將圖 Yun Tai Er Shih Pa Chiang Tu

Classification C 33

Subject

References

Author 清張士保畫 Ch'ing Chang Shih Pao

Edition 金陵張志瑢刻 Chin Ling Chang Chih Chü Block-Printing edition.

Index

Bound in 一冊　1 Tsê

Remarks 道光丙午年刊

Dated : Tao-Kuang "Ping-Wu" period

548

The University of Toronto Chinese Library
....

Accession No. 2378   Index No. 040-dcde

Title 宋李忠定公年譜 Sung Li Chung Ting Kung Nien Pu

Classification B 107

Subject

References

Author 清黃完中輯 Compiled by Huang Chai Chung.

Edition 三餘書屋叢書 San

Index

Bound in 1 Tsï

Remarks 竹紙 Bamboo paper.

The University of Toronto Chinese Library

· ·

Accession No. 2379   Index No. 024-fid

Title 南陽集 Nan Yang Chi

Classification D 33

Subject

References

Author 宋趙湘撰 ~~著~~ Written by Sung, Chao Hsiang.

Edition 武英殿聚珍版 Wu Ying Tien Movable-type edition

Index

Bound in 六卷一冊 6 Chuan 1 Tsé

Remarks 竹紙 Bamboo paper
夹板 wood-block.

550

551

Accession No. 2382   Index No. 037-a h l f

Title   太常遺草 Tai Ch'ang I Tsao

Classification   ~~呈毛~~ C338

Subject

References

Author   明 洪文衡著 Ming, Hung Wen Heng.

Edition   族脊漢楛刊本, 精刊
Tou Yi Hung Wu Block printing edition
(Fine-printed edition)

Index

Bound in   一冊   1 Tsê

Remarks   毛邊紙 Mao pien paper

The University of Toronto Chinese Library

. . . .

Accession No. 2383   Index No. 125-zze

Title 老子故 Lao Tzŭ Ku

Classification C33

Subject

References

Author 馬其昶述 Given in oral by Ma Ch'i ch'ang

Edition 抱潤軒周氏刊 Pao Jun Hsüan Chou Shih
                          Block-Printing edition

Index

Bound in 上下兩卷 一冊 2 chüan 1 Tʻao

Remarks 毛边纸 Mao-Pien paper
         夾板 wooden folder

553

Accession No. 2384　　　　　　Index No. 009-nzeg

Title 儒門法語輯要 Ju mên Fa yü Chi yao

Classification C33

Subject

References

Author 清彭定求原編　湯定釗輯要 *edited by* Ch'ing, P'êng Ting Chiu, Tang Ting Chao.

Edition 山東書局重刊本 Reprinted by Shan Tung Book Co.

Index

Bound in 一冊　1 Tsè

Remarks 附儒門法語夾板

The University of Toronto Chinese Library

. . . .

Accession No. 2385   Index No. 046-ikzz

Title 嵐漪小艸 Lan I Hsiao Tsao

Classification D23

Subject

References

Author 清 翁方綱 撰 Written by Ch'ing, Fên Kang.

Edition 南昌,使院鋟版 Nan Chang, Shih Yuan Ch'ien Blocks

Index

Bound in 一冊 1 Tsè

Remarks 竹紙 Bamboo paper

557

The University of Toronto Chinese Library

....

Accession No. 2388   Index No. 048-bdkc

Title 左忠毅公年譜 Tso Chung I Kung Nien Pu

Classification B 107

Subject

References

Author 明,左光斗 Ming, Tso Kuang Tou.

Edition 民國馬其昶纂 Compiled by Min Kuo, Ma Chi Chang.
桐城馬氏刊本,硃印 Tung City, Ma Shih block
print edition,
Red Printed.

Index

Bound in 上下二卷一册 2 chüan 1 tsê

Remarks 綿連紙. Mien Lien paper.

558

Accession No. 2389　　　Index No. 167-d e h g

Title 欽定修造吉方立成　Chin Ting Hsiu Tsao Chi Fang
　　　　　　　　　　　　　　Li Chêng

Classification B 307

Subject

References

Author 清欽天監編, *edited by Chin* Ch'ing, T'ien Chien

Edition 官版 offical-printed edition.

Index

Bound in 一冊　1 Tsê

Remarks 清光緒三十年製 made in, Ch'ing K.
　　　　　　粉紙. Powder paper.

The University of Toronto Chinese Library

....

Accession No. 2391   Index No. 046-gcyf

Title 島夷誌略 Tao I Chih Lüeh gcyf

Classification B 海 147

Subject

References

Author 元汪大淵撰 Written by Yüan, Wang Ta Yüan.

Edition 龍氏精刊 四庫全書本
Lung Shih fine-printed ed.

Index

Bound in 一冊   1 Tse

Remarks 光緒十八年刊 Block-engraving in 18th year of Kuang
綿連紙 Mien Lien paper   Hsü

Accession No. 2392   Index No. 149-99

Title 說教 Shuo Chiao

Classification C 731

Subject

References

Author 清 彭光譽 撰 (written by) Ch'ing, P'êng Kuang Yü

Edition 進呈本 Presented to the Throne.
文光齋刻版
Wen Kuang Chai Block-printing edition

Index

Bound in 一冊 1 Tsê

Remarks 綿連紙 Mien-Lien paper

The University of Toronto Chinese Library

. . . .

Accession No. 2393   Index No. 140-h f l

Title 菜根譚 T'sai Kên T'an

Classification C 328

Subject

References

Author 明洪應明 Ming, Hung Ying Ming

Edition 家藏版 Private-Printed ed.

Index

Bound in 一冊 I Tsé

Remarks 毛太紙 Mao Tai paper

The University of Toronto Chinese Library

. . . .

1529 P. 95

Accession No. 2374   Index No. 167-3½g

Title 金剛經 Chin Kang Ching

Classification C—513

Subject

References

Author 王大燮 Copied by Wang Ta-Hsieh

Edition 寫刻版,民國17年石印 Private family edition Home edition, dated Republic 17/1928. Lithrographic edition

Index

Bound in / 套, / 冊

Remarks

The University of Toronto Chinese Library

. . . .

Accession No. 2395   Index No. 032-lzfg

Title 墨子後語 Mo Tzu Hou Yu

Classification C 308

Subject

References

Author 清孫詒讓撰, Written by Ching, Sun I Jang

Edition 家藏版 Private-family printed edition

Index

Bound in 一冊 1 Ts'e

Remarks 綿連紙 Mien Lien paper
夾板 wooden-block folder

564

Accession No. 2396   Index No. 024 9ic

Title 南遊記 *Nan Yu Chi*

Classification B 227

Subject

References

Author 白齡 *Po Ling*

Edition 守意寵藏板 *Shou Yi Kan blocks preserved.*
嘉慶乙丑 *"Chia-ching" I chou"*

Index

Bound in 1 Tsè

Remarks

Accession No. 2397   Index No. 198-ʃ d k m

Title 皕宋樓藏書源流攷

Classification Li Sung Lou Tsáng shu Yüan Liu Kao
8117

Subject B 337

References

Author 王儀通 Wang Yi Tung

Edition 光緒年 Kuang-Hsü period.

Index

Bound in 1 Tsé

Remarks

566

The University of Toronto Chinese Library
....

Accession No. 2398   Index No. 061-3ff

Title 慈恩傳 Tzʻu En chuan

Classification 別7

Subject

References

Author 唐沙門釋 彥悰述 ~Tʻang, Sha Men, ~~Listed~~ ~~Translated~~ explained by

Edition 守意籠藏板 Shou Yi Kʻan Given in oral by Yen Tsung blocks preserved.

Index

Bound in 5 chüan, 1 Tsʻe

Remarks

The University of Toronto Chinese Library

. . . .

Accession No. 2400   Index No. 113-ℓ 2 p c

Title 禪林寶訓 Shan Lin Pao Hsün

Classification C 513

Subject

References

Author 釋淨善重集 Recollected by I Ching Shan

Edition 般若堂刻 Pan Jo Tang Block-engraving

Index

Bound in 四卷一冊 4 Chuan 1 Tsé

Remarks 竹紙 Bamboo paper

The University of Toronto Chinese Library

· · · · · · · · · · · · · · · ·

Accession No. 2401   Index No. 064 — 2 l c z

Title 抱潤軒文集 Pao Jun Hsüan Wen Chi

Classification D⁴³

Subject

References

Author 馬其昶著 Ma Ch'i Ch'ang

Edition 安徽官紙印刷局石印
An-hui Official Paper Publishing Co. Lithographic edition

Index

Bound in 九卷一冊 9 Chüan, 1 tse

Remarks 宣統元年印 1st Year of "Hsüan-Tung"
粉紙 Powder Paper —

The University of Toronto Chinese Library

. . . .

Accession No. 2402   Index No. 146-ggg

Title 西行日記 Hsi Hsing Jih Chi

Classification C-308

Subject

References

Author 清池仲佑撰 Written by Ch'ing, Ch'ih Chung Yu

Edition 商務印書館鉛印大字本
Commercial Printing Press Type-selling large
character edition

Index

Bound in 上下二卷一册
Remarks 2 Chüan, 1 Tsê
译纸
imported paper

570

Accession No. 2403   Index No. 109-2932

Title 真教自証 Chen Chiao Tzu Cheng

Classification C 251 971

Subject

References

Author 耶稣會晁德莅撰
Compiled by Ya Su Hui Chao Te Li

Edition 铅印本 Type-setting edition

Index

Bound in 一册 1 tsè

Remarks 油光纸 oil paper

. . . .

Accession No. 2404   Index No. 159-g d d f

Title 輕世金書 Chʻing Shih Chʻüan Shu

Classification C 13

Subject

References

Author 極西陽瑪諾譯 *Translated by:* Chi Hsi Yang Ma Nê

Edition 重刊本 reprinted edition

Index

Bound in 四卷一冊 4 Chüan, 1 tsê

Remarks 油光紙 Oil Paper

以上二種共一夾版 wooden folder

Accession No. 2405   Index No. 032—26d

Title 墨井集 Mo Ching Chi

Classification 戊33

Subject

References

Author 清吳漁山著 Ch'ing, Wu Yü Shan
Edition 土山灣印書館印 T'u Shan Wan Printing Press

Index

Bound in 五卷一冊 5 Chüan! Tsê

Remarks 宣統元年印 1st Year of "Hsüan-Tung"
油光紙 Oil paper

574

Accession No. 2407 稿   Index No. 039-mzi

Title 譬言編 Hsüeh Yen Pien

Classification D 33

Subject

References

Author 清吳伯尚著 Ch'ing, Wu Pai Shang

Edition 家藏版 Private-family edition

Index

Bound in 六卷一册 6 chüan, 1 ts'è

Remarks 毛边纸 Mao-pien paper bamboo paper

Accession No. 2409   Index No. 085-akgc

Title 永嘉郡記 Yung Chia Chün Chi

Classification B 222

Subject

References

Author 宋鄭緝之撰 Shu Sung, Cheng Ch'i Chih

Edition 清孫貽讓校集
Ch'ing, Sun I gang collected collations
石印本 Lithographic edition

Index

Bound in 一冊 1 tsè

Remarks 綿連紙 Mien lien paper

Accession No. 2410   Index No. 010-bbgb

Title 元也里可温攷 Yüan Yeh Li K'o Wen Kao

Classification B 117

Subject

References

Author 陳垣學 Chên Yitan Hsueh

Edition 新會陳氏刊 Hsin Hui Ch'ên Shih block ⟶ engraving
鉛印本 Type-setting edition

Index

Bound in 一册 1 tsè

Remarks 毛边纸 (Mao-pien) paper
bamboo

The University of Toronto Chinese Library

....

Accession No. 2411   Index No. 140-hkjg

Title 訄漢微言 Tao Han Wei Yen

Classification C 13

Subject

References

Author 清章炳麟述 given in oral by: Ch'ing, Chang Ping Lin

Edition 鉛印本 Type-setting edition

Index

Bound in 一册 1 tsé

Remarks 民國五年印 The 5th year of the Republic
绵連纸 Mien lien paper

The University of Toronto Chinese Library

. . . .

Accession No. 2412   Index No. 061—Cc zf

Title 忍耐子詩鈔 Jen Nai Tzu Shih Ch'ao

Classification 乃 68

Subject

References

Author 清王從龍著 Ch'ing, Wang Tsung Lung

Edition 鉛印 Type-setting edition

Index

Bound in 一冊 1 Tsê

Remarks 竹紙 Bamboo Paper

The University of Toronto Chinese Library
....

Accession No. 2413   Index No. 061—CCzf

Title 忍耐子詩鈔 Jen Nai Tzu Shih Ch'ao

Classification 女68

Subject

References

Author 清王從龍著 Ch'ing, Wang Tsung Lung

Edition 鉛印本 Type - setting edition

Index

Bound in 一冊 1 Tsé

Remarks 毛边紙 Mao Pien Paper
                    (bamboo)

Accession No. 2414   Index No. 007-3ydz

Title 二黃先生集 Er Huang Hsien Sheng Chi

Classification D 33

Subject

References

Author 清黃紹箕弟著 Ch'ing, Huang shao Chi Tzu

Edition 家藏版 郭博古齋印
Private-family edition

Index Printed by Kuo Po Ku Ch'ai

Bound in 一冊 1 tsê

Remarks 老也紙 Mao-pien paper
(bamboo)

Accession No. 2415   Index No. 018-mdyb

Title 劉壯肅公奏議 Liu Chuang Su Kung Tsou Yi

Classification B 72

Subject

References

Author 清劉銘傳撰 Ch'ing, Liu Ming Chuan.

Edition 鉛印本 Type-setting edition

Index

Bound in 一冊 1 ts'e

Remarks 洋紙 imported paper

Accession No. 2416   Index No. 128-klah

Title 聲調譜談龍錄 Sheng Tiao P'u Tan Lung Lu

Classification 石73

Subject

References

Author 趙飴山著 Chao I Shan

Edition 雅雨堂版 Ya yü Tang blocks
       寫刻本 Printed from copied edition

Index

Bound in 共三卷一四 3 chüan, 1 Tsé

Remarks 粉紙 Powder paper

The University of Toronto Chinese Library

....

Accession No. 2417   Index No. 077-ahbi

Title 正修上達 Cheng Haiu Shang Ta

Classification C 13

Subject

References

Author not given

Edition 松阱書屋藏版
Blocks preserved by Sung Feng Shu Wu

Index

Bound in 一册 1 tse

Remarks 光緒庚辰年刊 Dated "Kuang-Hsü" Kêng Chên
綿連紙 Mien lien paper

Accession No. 2418   Index No. 096-gmie

Title 理學辨似 Li Hsüeh Pien Szu

Classification C 13

Subject

References

Author 清潘子昭撰 Written by Ch'ing, P'an Tzu Chao

Edition 虞山潘氏叢書本
Yü Shan P'an Shih separate edition from
a collectanea

Index

Bound in 一冊 1 ts'e

Remarks 綿連紙 Mein lien paper

Accession No. ~~大中洲~~ 2421　　　Index No. 122 - ndjd

Title 羅近溪先生語要 Lo Chin chʻi Hoien Sheng yü yao

Classification　C-308

Subject

References

Author 清陶望齡輯 Compiled by ^Chʻing, Táo Wang Lin

Edition 江甯府城重刊
　"Chiang-Nin Fu Cheng reprinted edition"

Index

Bound in 一冊 1 tsʻé

Remarks 光緒二十年刊 The 20th year of "Kuang-Hsü"
　　毛慶代 Mao-pien paper

587

Accession No. 2423   Index No. 149-fjie

Title 詩韻辨字略 Shih Yün Pien Tzu Lüeh

Classification A 166

Subject

References

Author
Edition 沈定夫原刻 Original block printing edition by Shen Ting Fu.

黃倬重刊 Reprinted edition by Huang Cho.

Index

Bound in 五卷一冊 5 chüan, 1 tsê

Remarks 光緒三年刻 The 3rd Year of "Kuang Hsü"
竹紙 bamboo paper

588

The University of Toronto Chinese Library

....

Accession No. 2424   Index No. 053-2888

Title 庚子西行紀事 Keng Tzu Hsi Hsing Chi Shih

Classification B 222

Subject

References

Author 清唐晏纂 Compiled by: Ching, T'ang Yen

Edition 求恕齋刊 (block printing edition)
Chiu Shu Chai

Index

Bound in 一册 1 ts'e

Remarks 竹紙 bamboo paper

The University of Toronto Chinese Library

....

Accession No. 2425   Index No. 134-*l h m f*

Title 舊聞隨筆 Chiu Wen Sui Pi

Classification 乙 ~~13~~ /3

Subject

References

Author 清姚永樸撰 *Written by* Ch'ing, Yao, Yung P'u

Edition 鉛印本 Type-setting edition

Index

Bound in 四卷一册 4 Chüan, 1 Tsê

Remarks 毛边纸 Mao-pien paper

The University of Toronto Chinese Library
. . . .

Accession No. 2426   Index No. 160-38
Title 辛壬癸詩讅 Hsin Chiu I Shih Yin

Classification D 68

Subject

References

Author 欄柯叟撰 *Written by* Lan Ke Sou

Edition 蘇州振新書社印
Printed by "Su-Chou" Chen Hsin Book Company

Index

Bound in 三卷一冊 3 Chüan, 1 Tsê

Remarks 竹紙 bamboo paper

The University of Toronto Chinese Library
. . . .

Accession No. 2428   Index No. 104-rdpd

Title 癯翁叢抄 Chü Wēng Ts'ung Chao

Classification C 338

Subject

References

Author 清李庚長手抄 稾本

Edition Ching, Li Kēng Chang, copied from original edition
鉛印本
Type-setting edition

Index

Bound in 上下二卷 一册
2 Chüan 1 Ts'e

Remarks 毛边紙 "Mao-Pien" paper

The University of Toronto Chinese Library

. . . .

Accession No. 2429   Index No. 096-zzgb

Title 王文敏公奏疏稿 Wang Wen Min Kung Tsou Su Kao

Classification B 72

Subject

References

Author 清王懿榮撰 Written by Ching, Wang I Jung

Edition 江齋印刷廠排印 Type-setting by: "Chiang-Nin" publishing Company

Index

Bound in 一册 1 tsè

Remarks 綿連紙 Mien lien paper

593

The University of Toronto Chinese Library

. . . .

Accession No. 2430   Index No. 149-ld

Title 譚黔 Tán Ch'ien

Classification 史185 c 300

Subject

References

Author 清陳明遠撰 *Written by* Ch'ing, ch'en Ming Yüan

Edition 鉛印大字本 large character Type-setting edition

Index

Bound in 一冊 1 tsè

Remarks 綿連紙 Mien lien paper

594

The University of Toronto Chinese Library

· ·

Accession No. 2431   Index No. 069-inmg

Title 新疆禮俗志 Hsin Chiang Li Hsü Chih

Classification B 222

Subject

References

Author 王樹枏纂 *Compiled by:* Wang Shu Nan

Edition 陶廬叢書聚珍, 仿宋印書局印
Tao Lu separate edition from a collectanea
movable-type, Printing in Fang Sung Book Co.

Index

Bound in 一卷 一冊 1 chüan, 1 tsê
附新疆小正 一卷

Remarks 龍門紙 "Lung-Mên" paper

The University of Toronto Chinese Library

．．．．．．．．．．．．．．．．．．．．．．．．．．．．

Accession No. 2432   Index No. 097-3gpc

Title 瓜圃叢刊敘錄 Kua Pu Tsung Tan Hsü Lu

Classification ① * 73

Subject

References

Author 清金梁輯 Compiled by: Ch'ing, Chin Liang

Edition 家藏版 Private family edition

Index

Bound in 一册 1 tsé

Remarks 毛边纸 Mao pien paper

The University of Toronto Chinese Library

· ·

Accession No. 2433   Index No. 149-neh

Title 護法論 Hu Fa Lun

Classification C 308

Subject

References

Author 宋張商英撰 *Written by* Sung~~Sg~~, Chang Shang Ying

Edition 明初重刻元本 清撫刻
"Reprinted from original edition in early Ming"

Index

Bound in 一册 1 ts'e

Remarks 毛边纸 Mao-pien paper

597

Accession No. 2434   Index No. 167—mgcj

Title 鐵硯齋稿 T'ieh Yen Chai Kao

Classification D 3₃

Subject

References

Author 清汪吟龍著 Ching, Wang Yin Lung

Edition 翰寶齋鉛印
Han Pao Chai
∧Type-setting edition

Index

Bound in 一册 1 kie

Remarks 油光紙 Oil paper

The University of Toronto Chinese Library

....

Accession No. 2435   Index No. 039-m h &m

Title 學務平議 Hsüeh Wu P'ing Yi

Classification C 308

Subject

References

Author 清孫詒讓撰 ~Written by~ Ching, Sun I (Yi) Jao

Edition 瑞安廣明印刷局石印本
Shui-An Kuang Ming Pring Press lithographic edition
綿連紙 Mien lien paper

Index

Bound in 一冊 1 tále

Remarks

599

600

The University of Toronto Chinese Library

. . . .

Accession No. 2437   Index No. 169-d l l c

Title 開禧德安守城錄 K'ai Hsi Te An Shou Chêng Lu

Classification B 72

Subject

References

edited by:

Author 明王致遠編 Ming, Wang Chih Yüan

Edition 永嘉刻本
Yung Chia Block-printing-edition

Index

Bound in 一冊 1 tsé

Remarks 蘭味軒藏本 Preserved by Lan Wei Hsüan
竹紙 bamboo paper

Accession No. 2438   Index No. 163-2833

Title 鄰蘇老人年譜 Lin Su Lao Jen Nien P'u

Classification B 107

Subject

References

Author 清楊守敬自述 Ch'ing, Yang Shou Ching
                                   Given in oral

Edition 石印本 Lithographic edition

Index

Bound in 一冊 1 tsê

Remarks 綿連紙 Mien lien paper

The University of Toronto Chinese Library
....

Accession No. 2439   Index No. 162 - h g h f
Title 進修堂奏稿 Chin Hsiu T'ang Tsou Kao
                    75   187
Classification B72

Subject

References

Author 清白思佑撰 *Written by* Ch'ing, Pai En Yu

Edition 家藏版 Private - family ~~printed~~ edition

Index

Bound in 二卷一册 2 chüan, 1 ts'e
Remarks 光緒廿三年刻 *Block - printing edition*
The 23rd year of the Republic
綿連紙 Mien lien paper

The University of Toronto Chinese Library

....

Accession No. 2440   Index No. 118-e k 2 j

Title 笛渔小稿 Ti Yü Hsiao Kao

Classification D 33

510

Subject

References

Author 清朱昆田著 Ching, Chu K'un Tien

Edition 家藏版 ~~Home edition~~ Private ~~family~~ edition

Index

Bound in 十卷一册 10 chüan, 1 ts'e

Remarks 竹纸 Bamboo paper

604

. . . .

Accession No. 2441   Index No. 040-d z m z

Title 宋石，攀士詩集 Szu Shih Hsüeh Shih Shih Chi

449

Classification D 33

Subject

References

Author 李振綱校輯 Li Chên Kang Collected collations by.

Edition 家藏版 Private family edition

Index

Bound in 一冊 1 tsê

Remarks 夾板 wooden folder

605

Accession No. 2442   Index No. 010-d g k b

Title 先文勤公自訂年譜 Hsien Wen Ch'in Kung Tzu Ting Nien P'u

Classification B 107

Subject

References

Author 清王凱泰撰 Written by Ch'ing, Wang Kai Tai

Edition 家藏版 Private-family edition

Index

Bound in 一冊 1 tsè

Remarks 毛边紙 Mao-pien paper

Accession No. 2443   Index No. 173-P3○a

Title 靈言蠡勺 Ling Yen Li Shuo

Classification 311 297 470
C 13

Subject

References

Author 西人畢方濟撰 Written by Westerner, Pi Fang Chi

Edition 用四庫全書本鉛印 Type-setting edition

新會陳任校刊

Index Hsin Hui Chen Sheh collated edition

Bound in 上下二卷一册
2 Chüan, 1 Tsé

Remarks 毛边纸 Mao-pien paper

Accession No. 2444   Index No. 162-费思堂

Title 退思堂詩存 T'ui Szu Tang shih Ts'un

575 479

Classification ① 68

Subject

References

Author 周緒庠著 Chou Hsu Hsiang

Edition 同饗印刷所鉛印
Type-setting edition by:
Tung Hsin printing press

Index

Bound in 二卷一册 2 Chüan, 1 tsê.

Remarks 民國十二年印 Printed in the 12 year of
The Republic
毛邊紙 Mao-pien paper

Accession No. 2446   Index No. 037-ِ$ِ$ـ$

Title 大意尊聞 Ta Yi Tsun Wen

Classification B307

Subject

References

Author 清方東樹著 Ch'ing, Fang Tung Shu

Edition 家藏版 Private family edition

Index

Bound in 三卷一冊 3 chüan, 1 tsê.

Remarks Mao pien paper.

The University of Toronto Chinese Library

. . . .

Accession No. 2447   Index No. 109-d l

Title 肖墨 *Tun Mo*

Classification *B307*

Subject

References

Author 清湯霧纂 *Compiled by Ch'ing, T'ang I.*

Edition 家藏版 *Private family edition*

Index

Bound in 四卷一冊 *4 chüan 1 tsê*

Remarks 毛边纸 *Mao-pien paper*

....

Accession No. 2449   Index No. 061-*fikf*

Title 思福堂筆記 En Fu T'ang Pi Chi

~~124 140~~

Classification ~~603~~ B307

Subject

References

Author 清英和撰 *Written by* Ch'ing, Ying Hai

Edition 家藏版 Private ~~family~~ edition

Index

Bound in 二卷一册 2 Chüan, 1 ts'e.

Remarks 道光年刻 Dated: "Tao-Kuang" period
竹紙 Bamboo paper

Accession No. 2450   Index No. 172-kkd

Title 離憂集 Li Yu Chi

Classification 294 635 33 D14

Subject

References

Author 清 陳瑚 輯 Compiled by: Ching, Chen Hu

Edition 峭帆樓刻行 Engraved and distributed by: Chiao-fan Lou

Index

Bound in 二卷一冊 2 chüan, 1 ts'e

Remarks 毛邊紙 mao-pien paper

Accession No. 2451 教   Index No. 067-gdig

Title 救世新教綱教法 Chiu Shih Hsing Chiao Kang Chiao Fa.

Chiao

Classification C 731

Subject

References

Author 蔣尊諱敬署 Chiang Tsun Wei

Edition 鉛印本 Type-setting edition

Index

Bound in 1 tse

Remarks 毛边纸 Mao pien paper

Accession No. 2452   Index No. 011-9 b j 8

Title 俞曲園文續 Yü Ch'ü Yüan Wen Tü

Classification D 43

Subject

References

Author 清俞樾撰 Written by Ch'ing, Yü yüeh

Edition 春在堂原本石印
Chun Tsai Tang lithographic edition, original.

Index

Bound in 一册 1 tse

Remarks 東史紙 Lien-Shih paper

616

Accession No. 2453   Index No. 107-izd

Title 鼓山集 Ku shan chi

Classification 260 D 33

Subject

References

Author 清張寅著 Ching, Chang Yin

Edition 鉛印本 Type-setting edition

Index

Bound in 三卷一册 3 chüan 1 ts'é

Remarks 毛边纸 Mao-pien paper

The University of Toronto Chinese Library
....

Accession No. 2454   Index No. 073-hzeb

Title 曾文定公年譜 Tseng Wen Ting Kung Nien P'u

Classification B 107

Subject

References

Author 楊希閔編 edited by: Yang Hsi Min

Edition 三餘書屋叢書
San Yü Shu Wu separate edition
from a collectanea

Index

Bound in 一册 1 tsé

Remarks 竹紙 Bamboo paper

The University of Toronto Chinese Library
....

Accession No. 2455   Index No. 011-dzge
Title 金心經註解 Ch'üan Hsin Ching Chu Chieh

Classification C 圖 731

Subject

References

Author 松溪道人無垢註 Tao Jen Wu Kou
       Annotated by Sung Chi
Edition 昭慶寺大字經房慧空印造流通
        Printing in Chao Ching Szu Tai Tzu ^ Ching Fang Hui
        乾隆廿六年   K'ung.

Index The 26th year of "Ch'ien-Lung"

Bound in 1 Tse

Remarks

619